2017 | VOL. 1, Nº. 1

CAPACIOUS
JOURNAL FOR EMERGING AFFECT INQUIRY

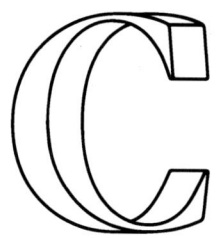

Capacious: Journal for Emerging Affect Inquiry Vol. 1 No. 1

Capacious is an open access journal and all content is licensed under a Creative Commons Attribution 4.0 International License (CC BY 4.0).

ISBN-13: 978-1547053117
ISBN-10: 1547053119

capaciousjournal.com

 You are free to copy and redistribute the material in any medium or format and remix, transform, and build upon the material for any purpose, even commercially. You must give appropriate credit, provide a link to the license, and indicate if changes were made. You may do so in any reasonable manner, but not in any way that suggests the licensor endorses you or your use.

Editorial team

CO-EDITORS-IN-CHIEF

Gregory J. Seigworth

Millersville University
Managing Editor
editor@capaciousjournal.com

Mathew Arthur

Vancouver School of Theology
editor@capaciousjournal.com

ASSOCIATE EDITORS

Wendy J. Truran

University of Illinois,
Urbana-Champaign
production@capaciousjournal.com

Bryan G. Behrenshausen

Red Hat
production@capaciousjournal.com

ca·pa·cious
kəˈpāSHəs/ 🔊

adjective
having a lot of space inside; roomy.

Capacious: Journal for Emerging Affect Inquiry is an open access, peer-reviewed, international journal that is, first and foremost, dedicated to the publication of writings and similar creative works on affect by degree-seeking students (Masters, PhD, brilliant undergraduates) across any and all academic disciplines. Secondarily, the journal also welcomes contributions from early-career researchers, recent post-graduates, those approaching their study of affect independent of academia (by choice or not), and, on occasion, an established scholar with an 'emerging' idea that opens up new avenues for affect inquiry. The principal aim of *Capacious* is to 'make room' for a wide diversity of approaches and emerging voices to engage with ongoing conversations in and around affect studies.

This journal will champion work that resists:

- the critical ossification of affect inquiry into rigid theoretical postures
- the same dreary citational genealogies
- any too assured reiteration of disciplinary orthodoxies

The journal will always encourage the energies and enthusiasms, the fresh perspectives and provocations that younger scholars so often bring to bear on affect within and across unique and sometimes divergent fields of intellectual endeavor. *Capacious* seeks to avoid issuing formal 'calls for papers' and 'special theme issues.' Submissions to this journal are accepted at anytime and are welcome to pursue any and all topic areas or approaches relating to affect.

Our not-so-secret wish is that essays and issues will forever remain capacious and rangy: emerging from various disciplines and conceptual [t]angles. Indeed, our aim for every journal issue would be that its collected essays not really coalesce all that much, but rather rub up against one another unexpectedly or shoot past each other without ever touching on quite the same disciplinary procedures, theoretical presuppositions or subject matter.

Capacious shall always endeavor to promote diverse bloom-spaces for affect's study over the dulling hum of any specific orthodoxy. From our own editorial practices down through the interstices of this journal's contents, the *Capacious* ethos is most thoroughly engaged by those critical-affective undertakings that find ways of 'making room.'

Gregory J. Seigworth
Mathew Arthur

July 2017

Editorial board

Ben Anderson
Durham University

Meera Atkinson
University of Technology Sydney

Joshua Trey Barnett
University of Minnesota, Duluth

Lauren Berlant
University of Chicago

Lone Bertelsen
University of New South Wales

Lisa Marie Blackman
Goldsmiths, University of London

Casey Boyle
University of Texas at Austin

Jack Bratich
Rutgers University

Sarah Cefai
University of Surrey

Rebecca Coleman
Goldsmiths, University of London

Ann Cvetkovich
University of Texas at Austin

Joe Deville
Lancaster University

Jennifer Fisher
York University

Radhika Gajjala
Bowling Green State University

Jeremy Gilbert
University of East London

Melissa Gregg
Intel Corporation

Lawrence Grossberg
University of North Carolina, Chapel Hill

Richard Grusin
University of Wisconsin – Milwaukee

M. Gail Hamner
Syracuse University

Alison Hearn
University of Western Ontario

Anna Catherine Hickey-Moody
The University of Sydney

Ben Highmore
University of Sussex

Tero Karppi
University of Toronto

Anu Koivunen
Stockholm University

Ali Lara
The City University of New York

Mona Mannevuo
University of Turku

Erin Manning
Concordia University

Belén Martin-Lucas
University of Vigo

Brian Massumi
University of Montreal

Shaka McGlotten
State University of New York, Purchase

Andrew Murphie
University of New South Wales

Jussi Parikka
University of Southampton

Susanna Paasonen
University of Turku

Carolyn Pedwell
University of Kent

John Protevi
Louisiana State University

Jasbir Puar
Rutgers University

Andrej Radman
University of Delft

Jason Read
University of Southern Maine

Jenny Rice
University of Kentucky

Michael Richardson
University of New South Wales

Tony Sampson
University of East London

Donovan Schaefer
University of Pennsylvania

Natasha Schüll
New York University

Kyla Schuller
Rutgers University

Hasana Sharp
McGill University

Steven Shaviro
Wayne State University

Chad Shomura
University of Colorado, Denver

Eliza Steinbock
Leiden University

Elizabeth Stephens
Southern Cross University

Kathleen Stewart
University of Texas at Austin

Kristin Swenson
Butler University

Marie Thompson
Lincoln University

Milla Tiainen
University of Helsinki

Virginia Villamediana
FLASCO

Isabel Waidner
Roehampton University

Julie Wilson
Allegheny College

Emily Chivers Yochim
Allegheny College

CAPACIOUS

Table of contents

INTRODUCTION
i *Capaciousness*
Gregory J. Seigworth

ARTICLE
1 *Casino Light*
Joey Russo

INTERSTICE
12 *Forgotten Rituals of Yearning*
Agnieszka Anna Wołodźko

Attempting the Embrace n°s 22 & 24
Claire Paugam

ARTICLE
19 *Extraordinary Happenings and Ordinary Affects*
Sabrina Lilleby

INTERSTICE
29 *Feeling Poetry*
Mercy Romero

ARTICLE
35 *On Manga, Mimetics and the Feeling of (Reading a) Language: Toward a Situated Translational Practice*
Gretchen Jude

INTERSTICE
52 *Flowers* and *A Tiny Library*
Ben Highmore

ARTICLE
57 *Do You Want Vaporwave, or Do You Want the Truth?: Cognitive Mapping of Late Capitalist Affect in the Virtual Lifeworld of Vaporwave*
Alican Koc

INTERSTICE
78 *Gayl Jones, Barricaded Feeling and Unstately Black Life*
Sarah Jane Cervenak

ARTICLE
83 *Coding Intensive Movement with Technologies of Visibility: Alien Affects*
Michael Lechuga

INTERSTICE
98 *Strange Air*
Mathew Arthur

ARTICLE
103 *When Dust Gets in Your Eyes: Researching the Taboo*
Fiona Murray

INTERSTICE
117 *Thimble Fingers* and *Feminist Hygiene*
Kay Gordon

AFTERWORD
120 *Everything Initiates*
Katie Stewart

Blood of My Blood, Claire Giblin, 2006
Acrylic on canvas, 30 x 40"

Capaciousness

Gregory J. Seigworth
MILLERSVILLE UNIVERSITY

Affect is rangy. That's a given. No surprise then: different disciplines and angles of academic inquiry will take affect (and affects) up in subtle and often dramatically different ways – hooray! Hence, it is not uncommon then that these disciplines and angles will often find themselves engaged in lively, sometimes unexpected, conversations around both traditionally cherished and newly inspired points of consonance and dissonance – more hooray! Crucially, what 'works' – or doesn't work – within, say, one explanatory-exculpatory framework might find experiential-experimental purchase in another framework of inquiry. And, yes, sometimes conflicts arise within the self-same framework (see, for instance, psychology): hello age-old internecine battles over the reach/over-reach and sense of modesty/immodesty conferred upon different criteria for valuing advancements in the humanities and social sciences. Without a doubt though, the very ranginess of affect acts as a substantial source of these intra-, inter- and cross-disciplinary tensions.

Given this, it is worth trying to find ways – when possible – to make these shimmering, perhaps spikey, moments of disciplinary interface into something that is illuminatingly-mutually productive and not talking-past-each-other into a combative void. But having said that, there is sometimes nothing quite like an invigorating debate around those procedures and processes and problematics that have come to animate and sustain a particular zone of recognizable inquiry: whether a discipline, a field, a practice, etc. Ultimately, the point is not to dissolve tensions by imagining that affect study will somehow magically turn into some kind of overarching über-discipline (as if!) or, even more basically, into a single multi-discipline-straddling methodology – because that ain't happening. Ever.

Perhaps the key question for affect studies when it comes to such relatively pesky issues as disciplinarity is merely this: how might any specifically-angled engagement with 'affect' precipitate a re-imagining of the thresholds and continually shifting weight-bearing presuppositions / procedures / objects / relations that give unique texture, shape & rhythm to any discipline's sense of capaciousness? How far might a given set of knowledge-practices and theories stretch at their boundaries and yet remain recognizably, albeit elastically, 'within the true' of their own singular historically-derived sets of practices and problematics? If affect and, consequently, the study of affect is capacious and rangy (and it is), then those specialized methods/practices & initiating presumptions that characterize any discipline offer a kind of necessary boundedness for the infinities of making-room that help give form(s) to force(s).

For me, this links up too with one of the more puzzling allergic reactions to affect theorizing in recent times; the study of affect is not only perceived, for some, as an unwelcome blurring of certain disciplinary boundaries and procedures but, more so, as an outright rejection or negation of such world-making fundamentals as 'consciousness,' 'intentionality,' 'cognitive,' the 'discursive,' the 'individual,' the 'linguistic,' the 'social,' the 'representational,' the 'human,' the 'personal' etc. etc. – after all, studies of affect have been known to attach a 'non-' and/or a 'pre-' prefix to these terms. With the affixing of the dash (-) of the non- / pre-, some have heard the opening of a gap: a rupture, a tear, a spacing, a kind of chasm. Cognitive here //-sever-// non-cognitive over there. Personal here //-sever-// pre-personal over there. As if grappling with affect is somehow done by way of a magical presumption of purity and un-contamination ["the body now free of the mind!"] or the production of sequence of neatly aligned separations ["slip the bonds of the discursive, join the pre-linguistic, and win a trip to non-intentionality!"].

To the first of these, I will simply note that 'non-' is not 'anti-' and that affect study does not – indeed, cannot – sustain its workings through negation or inversion or exclusion. Suffice it to say, this would violate affect studies' hard-earned (not necessarily hard-wired) capacities – the always making-room of 'to be affected' and 'to affect' – for capaciousness: its mode of attention to the 'more-than,' the 'other-than,' the 'different-than,' its attunements to what exceeds and what seeps from the atmospheres and folds of encounters. "As if the whole point of being and thinking is just to catch it in a lie," as Katie Stewart writes in the afterword to this issue. And this seems an apt reply to anyone who hears affect theory as caught up in some manner of performative self-contradiction – "Hey! First, you said 'non'- and then snuck it in through the back door!" Well, not exactly. Affect study uses 'non-' to show that the back door was never a door at all (back or otherwise). It is an immersive universe; forgo the standard entry points and exits, instead it's doors (and more than a few windows) all the way around. 'Non-' is not the evacuation of or the vacancy surrounding an existent-something (cognition, intentionality, human, et al), but the saturating/magnetizing circumambience of everything. Think of affect's 'non-' as a way to take note of this excess. Affect study then as excess-tentialism.

'Pre-' is similarly oft-misinterpreted. Before consciousness? Before the individual? Before the social? Etc. On the immediate face of it, these questions seem almost willfully naïve: sort of like shining a flashlight into the darkness that protrudes in front of such more steadily-lit entities. 'So, you wish then to insert your dim flashlight-findings before the more tried-and-true-and-trusted? And these faint pre-glimmerings will somehow invalidate or overwrite the understandings that we've gleaned about the workings of consciousness, the rights of the individual, the power of the social?' Admittedly, I am being over-dramatic here when actually the role of 'pre-' in the study of affect is rather low-key and modest (in much the same way that Nietzsche said that we should recall consciousness to its necessary modesty). Questions – like those posed at the head of this paragraph – presume that we know well-enough in advance what consciousness, the individual, the social (and more) already encompass; they assume that, when 'pre-' is added, it indicates something that applies before the coming-into-coherence of the individual, the social, the cognitive, the discursive. But the case is slightly other than this. 'Pre-' points to the co-constitutive nature of particular things such as consciousness, the individual, the discursive [etc.] along with what is supposed to fall out or recede into the background as the context / conditions of emergence. 'Pre-' signals the co-participation of a particular surfacing effect (like 'consciousness') and the wider fielding of its production. Perhaps it is not so curious then, when during an interview I asked Brian Massumi: 'Is there anything before affect?' He replies: "There is everything before affect: participation" (Massumi 2016).

It is as if, by way of 'pre-,' the same query that affect (in)famously asks of a body – 'what can it do?' – is likewise asked of the cognitive, the personal, the linguistic, the individual, the social. Because we don't yet know. 'Pre-' addresses the establishing of a recognizably coherent-enough actuality (say, the linguistic) while not letting go of the processes, conditions, and contexts that give contour / texture / rhythm to its arising (hence, the pre-linguistic). Thus, it yields, for example: the consideration of consciousness alongside the processes that produce the distinction between consciousness and its other(s). Or, in another instance of 'pre-,' it means considering the individual and the social alongside the processes that lead to their mutually exclusive [now turned inclusive] bifurcation.

If 'non-' is a ground-clearing maneuver that can afford studies of affect the opportunity to figure in the (often gradual, barely noticeable) seepages and excesses of more-than, other-than, different-than(-human / -intentionality / -representational etc.), then 'pre-' (individual/social/linguistic etc.) offers the perpetual alongsidedness of the processual. In brief, 'non-' says 'not only this but more' whereas 'pre-' maintains, over and over again, 'yes and… yes and … yes and…'

Because there are not any readymade steps to follow, no half-buried answers waiting to be uncovered, every project related to affect enacts yet another context and set of conditions to be unfolded anew. The question of affect modulates at every point of contact, relying – yes – upon quasi-steadying disciplinary and sensory mechanisms of investigation but also across the length and breadth of intersecting / diverging trajectories of matter and matterings.

Talking about affect divorced from any particular context is, let's just say, difficult. Perhaps not entirely pointless – after all, theories of affect do coalesce and vibrate and unfasten around shared pathways of situational emergence and fade – but if affect study is to be capacious (as I have maintained it must) then it cannot be closed down (as outlined above) around any specific disciplinary route or explicit set of step-by-step methods, or cleanly-scrubbed concept-clusters or rote performative gestures. Cast a wary eye upon anyone who tells you that they have located the *one way* that critical attention to affect should be pursued.

But perhaps a few capaciously-oriented parameters could be ventured …

At its most fundamental abstraction, I would argue – ready your wary eye! – that the study of affect works to provide a contextualized account of relationality (in-between-ness) and singularity (this-ness) at the same time: by never letting go of the scalar nature of vicinity (about-ness: micro/macro level of forces, histories, & present pressures) and the continuous gradience of intensities (forcefulness or the +/- sensate slope of alteration in the ongoing state-of-things). The body (a body) – bearing, materially & immaterially, all of its affecting 'non-'s and 'pre-'s as its own unique and modulatory sets of capacities and intransigencies – figures in as orienting trajectory or pathway, defined by its viscosity (pleated-ness: its rhythmic composition of stickiness and porosity).

CAPACIOUS

These features – inbetween-ness, this-ness, about-ness, and forcefulness + a body's pleated-ness – are not prescriptions for practice (hardly), but are more like zones or thresholds that fuzz in and out as they come to figure into one's accounting of affect (or affects) situationally. Sometimes – indeed, more often than not – slippery things & event-processes don't resolve themselves into neat little compartments and tidy vectors and right angles, and so the study of affect stakes out a place in the numerous incoherences that texturize a world. Recognizing that untangling or separating-out and critical distancing are not always the only or best available options, affect study frequently chooses to 'middle out' by wading into the ambient overdeterminations of existence and the energies that move (or impede, swerve, etc) bodies (of all kinds) in the very midst of their activity. Yes, this middling-out of affect study can often feel like a muddling-through ('That's it?! But where is, um, agency? We want theories that jump up, assert themselves, and knock things over'). But why shouldn't one modest aim of affect study be: to make or foster along, even if the barest ripple across the surface, a more expansive ongoing-ness (which is not to ignore those visceral moments in the present that need expansive resistance too). And while that is never enough (when it is ever enough?), it can be a start, this making room. This capacious-ness.

References

Massumi, B. (2016). Writing Space: Interviews. Interview with G.J. Seigworth. *WTF Affect*. Available at: http://wtfaffect.com/brian-massumi/. Accessed 1 July 2016.

Casino at Ahi Mohave Reservation, Laughlin, Nevada
Renjishino, 2007

Casino Light

Joey Russo
UNIVERSITY OF TEXAS AT AUSTIN

Casino Light pays attention to the incommensurable qualities of the ethnographic scene. It attempts to move through critique to composition as a manner of grappling with the "too-much" quality of a world that avoids pronouncements about subjects as categorically bound ethical actors operating under the duress of some overarching schema (like "Addiction" or "Global Capitalism" or "Depression"). It instead considers the qualities of the scene itself, what becomes emergent to the ethnographic eye in lists, asides, descriptions of sound and light and bodies, and the heaviness of a shared feeling. It evokes the casino, a place of chance encounters, with the chance encounters of observational methods. It experiments with stories told about the casino by interspersing them with moments of pause, puzzlement, and wonder.

KEYWORDS
affect, American South, casinos, composition, incommensurability

I.

The rural casino is marked mostly by the blatancy of its composition. Delta Downs, the casino where I spent the most time, lies just off I-10 in Vinton, Louisiana. Built as a racetrack in 1973, it is set back in an unlikely, depressed neighborhood of dilapidated tract homes, shining there like a blighted oasis. Its parking lot is vast. The interior stinks of cigarettes, buffet meats, and unidentifiable puddings with Nilla wafer crusts. The buffet caters to a variety of palates. Besides the attempt at regional fare (stagnant gumbos, shrimp étouffées), there are variations on ambrosia – obscure mid-20th century dinner party desserts such as Watergate salad, for instance: a pistachio pudding filled with pineapples and marshmallows. There is a faded sheen to the columns and mirrors, a depressed Vegas covered in a film of dust. A particular severity in the fluorescence lays each object and body bare, every flaw revealed. The elderly frequent Delta Downs; it is not the playground of drunken bachelorette parties or the boys' night chaos vibes of Vegas. There is no cavorting, no intoxicated whooping of youth. The garish feel of the place clashes with its clientele, like a Depression era Dorothea Lange photography exhibition in a funhouse in which two aesthetics converge miserably: realism splashed with pop art in a willfully anachronistic portrait. Rows and rows of old folks connected to their machines, some with a umbilical cord-like device attached to the console itself – a card on a chain inserted into the slot. Their vulnerabilities flicker beneath the violently pastel lighting and glow. It gives the place an atmosphere of desperate glitz. The way their lives loom in their faces, the practiced scowl now set like stone, backlit by neon. A grimacing lady in a walker slowly edging toward the buffet, traversing a scene adorned with animatronic parrots in plastic palm trees and soundtracked by whatever satellite radio station produces mid 90s alternative radio staples alongside contemporary auto-tuned country. The machines themselves produce looping aural fields that play against the backdrop of sound, clashing with it at intervals, constantly resetting. It is a wonder how the sense of calm, even apathy, prevails amidst this soundscape. The soundtrack to a *Wizard of Oz* slot machine cackles at the indifference; long dead Margaret Hamilton as Wicked Witch mocking their inevitable failures ("I'll get you, my pretty"), which is met with no change in the deadpan. The clanging of bells, the slide whistle of failure, and crunchy digitized fanfares are all wasted on the set stares.

CAPACIOUS

As Natasha Dow Schüll has noted, frequent machine gamblers are not necessarily "playing to win" (Schüll 2012, 2). That approach is found in the naiveté of the novice, optimistic in a new venture of chance. Seasoned gamblers situate themselves differently in relation to chance and its spaces; some navigate a particular kind of addiction – one that entrances them in the machinic activity and repetition of the gambling console, feeding their drive. Schüll characterizes the addicted machine gambler as playing within a modified death-drive framework: "It is not that the addict desires death as such…but that she desires release from the perturbing contingencies and uncertainties of existence" (Schüll 2012, 223). They have perhaps chuckled once or twice at the cartoonish impositions of the machines; but now, their poise seems to suggest, is not the time for laughter. Either we have passed the point in which this is fun or else we came here to suffer from the start. The jackpot is notional, the colors and sounds distracting. We come here to play the slots, to tune out to the patterns at work here, to cocoon ourselves in the "rinding up" (Stewart 2011, 450) of habits that these relationships engender. The rest is noise.

Bruno Latour makes the case for a "compositionist" style of writing (2010, 473) that he positions in opposition to critique; critique, he argues, is always searching for the larger foundational truths under everything which it takes as its obligation to uncover. Critique in this way always has a particular valence towards the unearthing of what lies beneath. This critical practice, which flourishes for instance in anthropological writing, operates on a presuppositional model. What is seen is false, and through a systemic ethnographic practice, the veils of falsehood are removed so the system can be effectively diagnosed. However, that ethnography has always been an affective model should at this point come as no surprise. It is, after all, based on a sort of arcane evaluative process: the ethnographer, in an encounter with the field, armed with various presuppositions and hypotheses, nevertheless experiences a feeling that guides the manner in which they depict what is seen. The immersive experience of repeatedly encountering this feeling as it develops and solidifies into 'knowledge of the customs of x' for instance, is the basis of ethnographic certainty and deals with the notion of scientific replication in a much more unwieldy way. This is due to the notion that a repeatedly observed ritual is an open event – it is not isolated within particular laboratorial schema: it is vulnerable to the impingement of feeling. That feeling, how it is composed, structures the 'subjective' nature of what we have come to categorize as the qualitative. The ethnographic scene thus instantiates a moment in which the state of the ethnographer blends productively with the feeling of a field, an apprehending or harnessing of affect. The compositional quality of the ethnographic scene, in this sense, is meant to be a blueprint for how things affectively fall into place. The sequence of events, what is dwelt upon, and the framing of character seem to anticipate a reader whose eyes will adjust to the light the ethnographer saw in a shared epiphany. Foundational ethnographic work become inextricable from the lasting play of iconic scenes and symbols revealed within them: the bloody plumage of Geertz's cockfight, Boas' harsh winter and the rush of the sled, Firth's Tikopia clambering over the side of his ship, the laughter of Mead's unashamed tropic, the arrows of the Yanomamo turned on Chagnon. Where the roving ethnographic eye lands, and what it puts together, has long been a concern of anthropological understanding. The writerly touch bolsters the integrity of observation and the refinement of the gaze depicted in that writing produces a clearer composition in which to walk around. We look through the eyes of the observer who, in retroactively constructing their own gaze, anticipates how we will look, with them, through them, at what was observed. This is the falling into place of composition; the play between what the ethnographer 'makes' and what she 'encounters'.

The composition of the rural Louisiana casino reveals mostly Deep South old timers, many of them working-class retirees, bussed in from assisted living homes and senior centers across Southeast Texas and Southern Louisiana. They come as hunting clubs, taxidermy clubs in RealTree vests emblazoned with their club logos, church groups freshly back from a cruise with tropical themed crucifix t-shirts and orthopedic beach sandals. They are fed at the buffets, they are sent vouchers to stay in the hotel rooms and attend the races. They are sent pamphlets that depict young, apparently wealthy and cosmopolitan people smiling beatifically at blackjack tables. A fair percentage of them are in wheelchairs or Rascals or have oxygen tanks, or both. They are practically all smoking, oxygen tank or no. There is live music in the evenings. They dance carefully, or sit at the tables bobbing their heads along to the slick band doing covers in a style that wouldn't be out of place on *The Voice*. The casino is depicting something, a composition of flashing lights and a maddening aural field of repeating musical phrases and sound effects. It is a meeting place of kitschy design and finely tuned practicality. Every machine is a manic loop contributing to the cacophony *en masse*, "a thousand electronic ringtone-like bleeps and bells – the sound of the ceaseless slots – replace clock time and the shift from diurnal to nocturnal life with an unremitting temporality of the ever present." (The Project on Vegas 2015, 229) Digitized voices from the machines' human or near-human characters come in a variety of strange stereotypes that encourage, scold, or mock. They might have a three second repertoire of movement that engages at a moment of loss or victory:

CAPACIOUS

stirring a cauldron, spinning a lasso, pulling a switch that sends a trolley over the cliff, the leopard leaping from the undergrowth. There are cowboys whooping as the stampede starts again ("Heeeere we go, y'all!"), witch doctors throwing hexes, Easter Island Moai that unlock doors in affectless baritone. A bikini-clad woman blows a kiss and the heart that issues from her mouth sets the loop in motion again. There are five-second jingles and the sounds of explosions overlaid with the *ka-ching* of the money drawer, the sound of coins clattering. Cash falls down in a deluge, wiping the screens in a queasy money-green wash. And then it all starts back up again.

One of the tasks of the ethnographer is to grapple with the incommensurable qualities we encounter in these compositions that seem not to fit together, but which nevertheless unfold before us. Often situated as the clash of radical worlds (Povinelli 2001) with normalizing and violent regimes of power, the value of incommensurability is a symbolically loaded relation. It is not just a moment of pointing out that things do not fit, but describes a relation by which ideological/political conflicts result from an aberrant presence of some sort. It points towards that presence that is always configured to make the State show its hand again, as it were. The version of incommensurability explored here dwells within the heart of that specter of hegemonic forms, the American South, rather than focusing on the effects of global capitalism's spread. I focus on the South, specifically Southeast Texas, as an epicenter, arguably the place where some of U.S.'s hegemonic forms fiercest supporters reside in the form of staunchly conservative publics, small towns whose modes of commiseration still foreground the most serious fundamentalisms, and hate group rallies where white supremacist ideologies are performed in what has become an unfortunate iconic regional scene. The observational quality of this work seeks not to make legible a distant society but to dwell in the thrall of unfamiliarity that results from gazing at some mundane object for too long and losing its meaning in the process. The scenes are quintessentially American, as seen by an American, which is to say they enjoy a certain banality in our popular culture. But they lose the banality of their composition, as anything regular tends to do after time spent mulling over it. My version of things not adding up slows down the notion of incommensurability to focus not on ruptures of the social, but something as quotidian as a casino where everyone appears to be sad - a strange composition that gives me pause. It is a sense of things being off that does not sit squarely with the feelings of enjoyment that such a space is ostensibly designed to convey. "Shouldn't we be happy here?" It starts not with big questions like "how does this public clash with the State?" but the observation that "something is happening here."

It starts with people whose being seems raw or wounded or scorched, especially at sunrise when the daylight floods in and embarrasses the spectacle in morning. Then the effects of the lights are not as intense; the scene is more exposed, somehow guilty. Many have been sitting at the same machine through the night and cannot be bothered to stop now for breakfast. Their bodies look pained, but hanging on. They look unwilled in the absorption of their practices. Some of them have little fetishes or lucky bits of seemingly random matter lined up along the video poker machines, dolls or action figures or old matchbooks. They execute hand gestures, flitting their fingers about in front of the screen or waving in a controlled motion: up, left, down, up, left, down. Then they pull the crank or press the Bet button. These gestures bring luck; they are brought off with precision and seem to want something. They seem to want to reduce the chances of failure, pulling the possibility of failure from the very air. As Schüll explains: "the control they experience, constricted as it may be, affords them a chance to change their relationship to loss – not by stopping or reversing it but by performing it themselves" (Schüll 2012, 216). The algorithms of the pseudo-random number generators dazzled for a moment, perhaps, their efficiency clouded by this ritual. I see a woman cock her head to one side and lift one hand while pulling deeply from a cigarette as if to say "what does it matter?" There is a shared affect: it feels like a bodily knowledge that one is exposed, one is making oneself known in this display. They labor here at the machines, their bodies at work for a purpose that is never quite worked out. One man notices me staring, and elbows me in the ribs, laughing: "They ought to walk around with 'Fuck Me' written on their forehead!" But here he is too of course. Here we both are. "Hey that one was rough," he says, as a particularly decrepit gambler limps past. A silence starts to spread between us as gambler after gambler walks past to the restroom. Mockery refuses to encompass the feeling of this place; incredulity gives way to exhaustion. We part ways, almost as though we have together committed some indiscretion.

Rather than try to make sense of the actions of those around me participating in the activities of the casino, I attempt here to sit with the impressions left from the repeated experience of witnessing events that seemed incommensurable to me on a number of levels. For me, the first question of ethnography is the interplay of simultaneous affective states: those that are observed and those that influence the trajectory of observation. Insofar as affect is transmittable or harnessable as a force that might manifest in shared experience (Brennan 2004), it is from which affective state the ethnographer attunes to that other considerations and frameworks emerge. This itself is a sort of gamble; it is a roll of the dice how one might feel on any given day. Ethnography, like sitting down at a slot machine, is an aleatory event. So to witness the actions of gamblers in an apparent state of apathy whose participation in these ritualized actions seem almost painful, is to wrestle with the incommensurable qualities in the composition of place. I spend time considering the physicality of the gamblers' bodies in these environments: how they sit in front of the machines, how their faces look, how the light illuminates and distorts them. Much different than the idea of market consumers displaying exuberant dispositions (Appadurai 2011), the shared state of the gamblers at my Louisiana casino enacted the appearance of an almost unwilled state. A well-rehearsed explanation for this condition, which centers the pull of capitalism, might cast the gamblers as automatons of capital's seductive machination. Repeated failures within an addictive market might not change the actions of its participants; it might merely change their attitudes toward participation, the Marxist argument goes. They continue to participate because they simply 'cannot help themselves', bereft of the spirit required to resist or object to their own manipulation. Without disregarding the idea that manipulation of feeling is undoubtedly involved in this phenomenon, I insist that this is more complicated than simply the sad reality of the 'zombies of capital' acting against their own best interests. I attempt to sit with the stories and the building of character that emerges in such a place; stories in which often very poor people save up their pennies to play the penny machines every week, blow their SSI checks on a few pulls of a lever, eat one of their only square meals of the week at the casino buffet, and come back to do it all again tomorrow.

The atmosphere of place and the specificities of a region matter when we are analyzing the supposedly homogenized spaces of capital: the rural casino of the Deep South has a different atmosphere than the casinos of the Las Vegas Strip; this is not an essentialist treatment or a caricature; it is taking seriously the idea of a critical regionalism (Powell 2007). Despite the insistent argument of homogenization's effects on a place like the United States, the intention of the ethnographer is to draw out the singular qualities of affects and characters across different regions. Here, what is sought is not some set of underlying reasons that explain why people gamble, but instead an attunement or bearing witness to people in a shared feeling, a composition that they remain wrapped within, might not be able to disconnect from, or in whose processes of manipulation they might not even actively participate. As Schüll observes, gamblers stuck in "the zone" present a deep portrait:

> What clues to collective predicaments and preoccupations might we find in this solitary, driven form of existence, caught between the everyday world and the otherworldly state of the zone?...it becomes possible to track how

> shared social conditions and normative behavioral ideals contribute to shaping gambling addicts' seemingly aberrant 'machine lives,' and to discern in those lives a kind of immanent critique of broader discontents. (2012, 190-191)

This last speculation is important, because it asks us to consider if there is a moment in which the accrual of a shared feeling, like exhaustion or cynicism, might generate a different relationship to the ill effects of capitalism, such as a gambling addiction. It asks us to think about the stuck agencies of those that are no longer actively falling into something; those that might have a fatigued and blunted relationship towards the always-disappointing trajectory of cruel optimism (Berlant 2011) in the scene that they find themselves wallowing.

II.

The remoteness of Southeast Texas lends itself to the lonely effects of vast expanses. Driving down the rural highways with nothing to encumber the view, the sky is big. The horizon comes right down to your feet. The sound of eighteen-wheelers comes in waves, punctuating the underlying hum of cicadas in the summer. The call of the casino has a different effect here than it might in an urban center. It is like a beacon whose signal reaches out into the darkness and drabness of the refinery zones, the depressed piney woods and backwaters. It is the one thing to do. One summer, the pull of this call is especially strong. We noticed it in the excess of commercials for the area casinos on TV: Delta Downs, Coushatta, L'Auberge, Harrah's, or The Golden Nugget. We noted the lines of cars in the parking lots, RVs and pickups pouring out into the street, overwhelming the neighborhoods. The casino billboards on the highways featuring a glowing Terry Bradshaw or advertising some "blast from the past" concert, .38 Special or Bachman-Turner Overdrive, vivid against the austere backdrop of scorched loblolly pines and kingdoms of petrochemical refineries. My best friend and I are staying with his folks out in Kirbyville, Texas in the Big Thicket, on one of the rural highways that lead deeper and deeper into the dread of the piney woods. Gambling addictions run in his dynastic Texan family, among other peccadilloes mentioned in hushed asides around campfires or when photo albums are dusted off, and we treat these habits with suspicion and a little pity. But time in the country propels the body into things. We are curious to see how they spend their evenings; we are under the thrall of profound boredom after just a week of wandering about looking for herons.

One morning, quite early, his Aunt J calls up and asks if we would accompany her to Delta Downs ("Delta", she calls it) not far across the Texas border. We agree, and she drives down to retrieve us at breakneck speed on these backcountry roads with the entitlement of a sheriff's wife, as she in fact is one - her late husband having been the Beaumont chief of police. Locals call these narrow roads "pig-trails". She comes down from a tiny town by the Sam Rayburn Reservoir where she lives alone in a 1970s style A-Frame house by the water. She is rail-thin, with classy red glasses and the kind of generalized matronly haircut that is common among white women of a certain age in the South. She chain-smokes Monarchs or Doral 100s in impossibly long drags like a sailor or a cowboy and coughs incessantly; she tells us the COPD isn't going anywhere and the breathing treatments don't help. She knows a lot about the area and history and the U.S. and state parks and the history of the police. She is hungry for talk, for company. She treats us with the sort of respect and almost professional courtesy reserved for salesmen of a bygone era. She refers to us as "the boys" in a sort of conspiratorial way, like we are rare birds. There is something practiced in it, a kind of distance in the courtesy. This is a mode of sociality in Texas, in which what might elsewhere be mistaken as coldness or distance passes comfortably as a measured and polite care. People are giving you your space, and that is to be commended. I like to think that Aunt J enjoys inhabiting certain memories in us, sliding back into the way she used to speak to her older brother Chuck who owned the gay club in Beaumont. I think of them working it out as kids. Two short, bespectacled children of foggy gender, the older siblings of a massive working class family. Treating him as a rare bird, too – a young man who didn't fit. Chuck has macular degeneration now and is considered legally blind. He lives next door to the house they grew up in, having lost all his money on "gambling and boys". We joke that he is like William S. Burroughs without the typewriter. He still drives to the casino regularly to gamble on the penny machines. The siblings chuckle and call him Mr. Magoo but he might die out there one day or kill someone and they know this. "But you cain't tell him nothin'," they say. When Chuck comes to the casino, he heads straight for the penny machines. His refrain is a repeated hum in three descending notes, *bmp, bmp, bmp*. But he stays home this time.

Aunt J changes once she enters the doors of Delta. She turns off conversation, spends the day smoking Monarchs and not budging from her machine. She doesn't drink alcohol, barely bothering to wave off the bright waitresses who float about in a sort of mania. After some hours we run into another of my friend's aunts, Dee, who is the physical opposite of Aunt J: completely round, with twinkly eyes and another haircut that hasn't changed much: a salt and pepper almost-mullet with feathered, short bangs. Her cigarettes are filterless Pall Malls, blunt and short. And Dee is on her way out, having spent the morning, so we decide to leave with her. Dee walks with a cane, having been injured in a fall at her hospital job years before; she has been gambling away the court settlement ever since. She says ribald things about women but tells us she doesn't have desire like that anymore, getting sad and a distance coming into her eyes as she recounts a few words about a long past girlfriend. Somebody crazy, something set on fire. A hand punched through glass. A scar. Aunt J and Aunt Dee are both addicted to gambling, meeting up here almost randomly, but knowing it is a strong possibility you might run into one of your ten siblings. They greet each other in a sidelong fashion, both in their own ways – jokes building up behind their eyes. Dee with a little twinkle and open mouthed smile. Aunt J all business, purse on lap, sat erect at the machine, mouth tight and making little grunting sounds of certainty, punctuating the progress of the machine's beeps and flashes, secure in its little functions of swindling and inhabited by its strange avatars.

It wasn't until the following morning that Aunt J stopped back at our place, fatigued and resigned. She had been in the casino for twenty-four hours. She had lost quite a bit of money. She had a sort of film covering her skin – she said she hadn't moved all night and hadn't taken a hotel room or eaten anything or drank any water. She just sat there smoking and hitting buttons, not even one of the all-nighters with the figurines or hand-wavers. No colorful visors or fun church club t-shirts. No taking enjoyment in the gambling. Just a perpetual duel with the machines, a tempering of the aleatory. "…machine-accelerated speed is a way to run ahead of the surprise and catch moments of chance—a way to be in charge of chance" (Schüll 2012, 219). In the moment of pressing the Play button, the life exposes itself to a definite possibility. As if losing in here might protect us from losing out there, a type of arcane contingency plan. It wasn't the first time Aunt J had spent all night in the casino; Dee had told us about another of her benders at Harrah's in New Orleans, when J had returned to their hotel room in the morning, spent and defeated. It was just after her husband had died, a long and painful struggle with leukemia. Dee described Aunt J as appearing to have shrunk overnight and changed color. She sat dejected in a chair before them, exposed to them, the composition of her. Here I am. Here is what has become of me. Dee said: "She was green, like money."

References

Appadurai, A. (2011). The Ghost in the Financial Machine. *Public Culture* 23 (3), pp. 517–539.

Berlant, L. (2011). *Cruel Optimism*. Durham: Duke University Press.

Brennan, T. (2004). *The Transmission of Affect*. Ithaca: Cornell University Press.

Latour, B. (2010). An Attempt at a "Compositionist Manifesto". *New Literary History* 41 (3), pp. 471-490.

Powell, D.R. (2007). *Critical Regionalism: Connecting Politics and Culture in the American Landscape*. Chapel Hill: University of North Carolina Press.

Povinelli, E. (2001). Radical Worlds: The Anthropology of Incommensurability and Inconceivability. *Annual Review of Anthropology* 30, pp. 319-334.

Schüll, N. (2016). Abiding Chance: Online Poker and the Software of Self-Discipline. *Public Culture* 28 (3), pp. 563-592.

Schüll, N. (2012). *Addiction by Design: Machine Gambling in Las Vegas*. Princeton: Princeton University Press.

Stewart, K. (2011). Atmospheric Attunements. *Environment and Planning D: Society and Space* 29 (3), pp. 445-453.

Stewart, K. (2010). Worlding Refrains. In: M. Gregg & G. J. Seigworth, eds. *The Affect Theory Reader*. Durham: Duke University Press., pp 339-353.

The Project On Vegas. (2015). *Strip Cultures: Finding America in Las Vegas*. Durham: Duke University Press.

Forgotten Rituals of Yearning

Agnieszka Anna Wołodźko (Text)
LEIDEN UNIVERSITY

Claire Paugam (Images)

> My mouth, main entrance of my body,
> my open-to-the-world cave full of precious stones
> shining with sunlight.
> I will never get to know all the colors of my hidden world,
> this ocean I cannot [dive] deep into and discover the richness of its underwater flora.
> And suddenly the cycle repeats itself:
> everything which was outside becomes a part of me
> but just for a moment.
> What is taken from the outer place to your inner kingdom
> has to be given back.
> The inland of mine I can touch and see is this wide opened mouth
> yearning for the outside world.
>
> — Claire Paugam, *Attempting the Embrace n° 22*

"Yearning: a word stemming from Afro-American spirituality, which passes from text to text, gives the appropriate tone for this experimentation. It conjugates hope, the plaintive cry and desire; that for which the soul, at one and the same time, has a thirst and does not have the power to define what it thirsts for. Yearning is something that transforms the soul, not something that defines what the soul has to appropriate" (Pignarre and Stengers 2011, p.48).

Once there were witches, not long ago, still present in the forgotten lands of Poland called "Szeptuchy." In English, *szeptucha* would be close to the word "whisperer". The custom was that once you repeated a particular sequence of words in contact with the ill body, the words will heal this body. The belief in

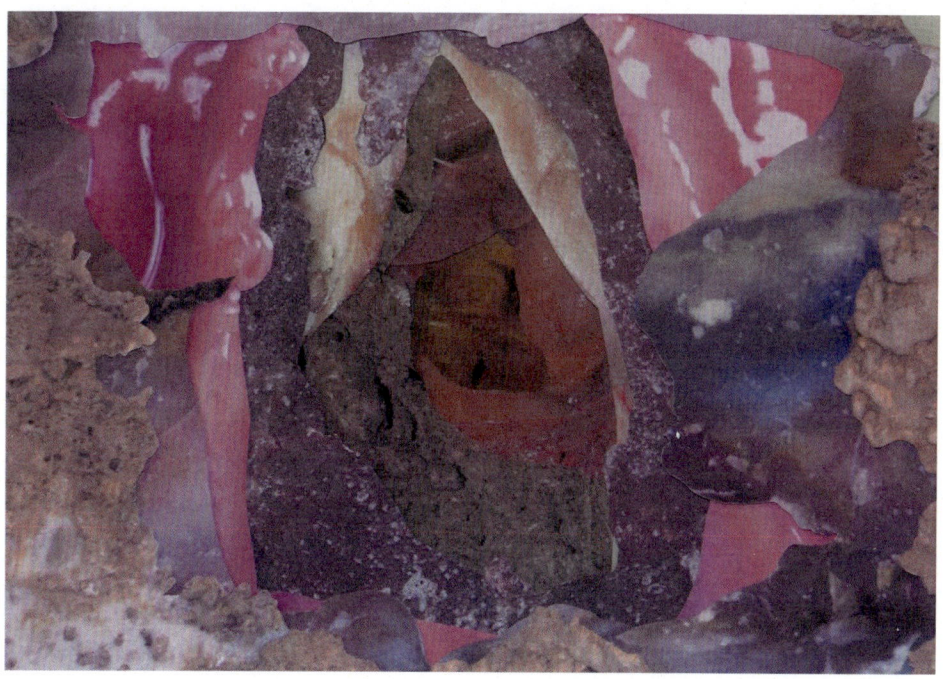

Attempting the Embrace n° 22, Claire Paugam, 2015
Sheets of glass, photographs, 40 x 40cm

the actual material transformation through soft whispering and repetition was nothing extraordinary, it was rather a part of life, although secret and ascribed only to peasant, uneducated women.

I was often sick when I was a child, and the visits to the doctor were regular. I remember once, however, that my grandmother made me drink an herb tea after whispering something to it, a strange ritual called "zamawianie." I was told that it was a sort of a prayer, and the mocking tone of the rest of the family discouraged me from further inquiry about what she had actually done. Only later, when it was too late to ask my grandmother, I found out that her mother, my great grandmother, was a known local "witch", to whom many from the neighboring villagers would travel to get healing.

Isabelle Stengers writes that we, women in "rational science", find ourselves to be amnesic (Stengers and Despret 2014, p. 1924). We forgot about the witches of the past and their collective knowledge gathered outside our institutions; women working in the fields, through risky, windy encounters, embodying the dirt of daily life. Women healers: those that had a deep understanding of the relational, material embedding of each encounter that transforms. It seems today that those who continue the struggle, the yearning for attachment despite unknowns; those who oscillate between the two words – the real and speculative, the material and immaterial, human and non-human, blurring established boundaries between them – are the witches of the present performing the witchcraft of art.

The knowledge of relations of transformation and collective gathering, the yearning for movement, Deleuze and Guattari ascribe to witchcraft and the rituals of sorcerers. As they write:

> When demonology expounds upon the diabolical art of local movements and transports of affect, it also notes the importance of rain, hail, wind, pestilential air, or air polluted by noxious particles, favourable conditions for these transports. Tales must contain haecceities that are not simply emplacements, but concrete individuations that have a status of their own and direct the metamorphosis of things and subjects. (Deleuze and Guattari 2004, p. 288).

Demonology here regards the relations of movements and intensities that generate bodies by their transformation and mutation in the encounter. Such practices of transformation in the encounter are not only of the past, but also of the future-present captured in the "demonic" practice of art, in its production and preservation of affects and percepts. "A compound of perceptions and affects" (Deleuze and Guattari 1994, p. 164), is preserved in art but, as Deleuze and Guattari argue, "if art preserves it does not do so like industry, by adding a substance to make the thing last" (1994, p. 163). Preservation does not render things fixed, does not capture them in their instability. On the contrary, what art preserves is that which cannot be captured, what belongs to a moment but not to identities or particular bodies. What art preserves, according to Deleuze and Guattari, is affects and percepts, where affects are understood not as feelings but transformations of feeling, and percepts not as perceptions but transformations of ways of seeing (1994, p. 164).

These movements of relations of transformation: of rain, hail, wind and air, are like the movement of the

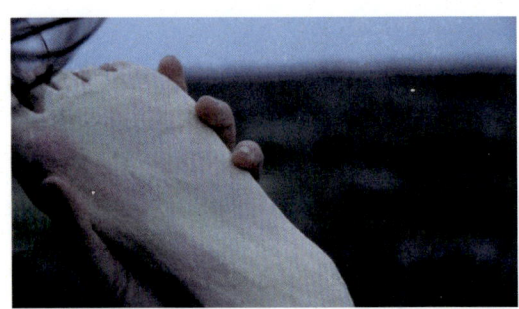

first elements that condition all other transformations. Here, affect produced in the encounter would become another element, as a condition of all creation and mutation. In my native Polish, the word for classical elements is *żywioły*. *Żywioł* derives from the word *życie* which means life. Beside the philosophical meaning of classical element, it can denote a vast, powerful and sudden "natural" event that is independent from will. *Żywioł* can also mean a group

Attempting the Embrace n° 24 Claire Paugam, 2015
Video, 02:58 (above, left, and following page)
clairepaugam.com/attempting-the-embrace-n-24

of people generating a gathering and an element of contents – it can denote both a capacity and meaning. Somehow, the affective nature conveyed by the Polish word *żywioł* captures Deleuze and Guattari's demonic description: as non-personal, generative, transformative, and collective understanding of movement. To produce and practice affect understood as a phenomenon, an event that cannot be captured but only lived through, in its paradox and impossibility becomes a "diabolical art" or what Isabelle Stengers named as "the art of the witches" (2013, p 196).

Claire Paugam's artistic rituals titled "Attempting the Embrace" perform the mattering of stones into flesh, and flesh into stones (Paugam 2014-2017). They are the rituals of transformation through a visual analogy that bring bodies into an encounter of their mutual transformation. Each episode of this attempt

 whispers the sound of wind, only to be interrupted by the sound of breaking flesh on the stones of the earth. She whispers with the sound of crashing body parts, when her teeth and tongue chew the porous skin of the minerals. Without any *ressentiment* or romanticization, she performs the ritual of mattering, of movement and relation searching for the elements, for transformation. Her work captures earth, dirt's transversal wondering. These are affects as encounters through which bodies are generated and transformed. By means of representation, she changes signification into significance, and like a Stengers' witch, she mutates and brings bodies into movement, into mattering.

In her art installations, the visual analogy between the flesh and the stone of the earth does not signal, unlike allegory, that which is lacking. Unlike allegory which veils ideas and strengthens differences, Paugam's use of visual analogy is carnal and actual. She does not reveal differences in order to overcome them by bringing them to a balanced unity. Rather she accelerates those differences by producing new bodies that are transformed by their encounter. Analogy as such does not communicate what already exists; it is not a bridge between two opposites. Rather it exposes visibly what it communicates; it has "its ability to make things actually get together…, resembles the affinity-producing efficacy of a charm or amulet." For Barbara Stafford, analogy is like "sexual reproduction" in which the third new concept arises bridging the two opposing ones (Stafford 2001, p. 175). I would, however, argue that analogy as practiced in Paugam's work, rather than resembling dialectic relation, produces a new relation by multiplying already existing ones. By stretching the moment of encounter between bodies, she practices the processes of differing – it is the magic of creating, and continuing transformations without the need of finding any third, distinct way.

Analogy understood as encounter within transformation is something distinct from allegory that presupposes the radical, because essential, difference between bodies; difference that is based on the priority of fixed identity. Rather than connecting what is believed to be separated, analogy explores connections and relations between bodies that are already related by the encounter. In Paugam's installations, analogies of flesh and stone become actual bodies meeting that which would not otherwise be seen. "Seeing, seeing what happens" as Deleuze and Guattari would say, becomes here a carnal, bodily experimentation (1994, p. 128). Talking about the body in non-dualistic terms requires this notion of the visual, bodily reciprocity, and analogy that endeavors to find similarities, mutual affections and resonances that persistently differs.

Through analogy Paugam searches for lost encounters; forgotten and undesired meetings of bodies, flesh, and dirt of earth. In her work, she practices yearning for the continuous search for mutations, for making close what has always already been within you but escapes your notice, like the unwanted thought that makes you go where you do not want to. The outside yearning, that never has been, that is yet to come, become(s) you. Her installations are populated by such encounters; human, but mostly non-human, bodies as already practicing the collective witchcraft of transformations. And like words, her images transform and mutate the bodies. Unlike, however, any word, Paugam's visual analogies not only transform but generate spaces where non-human words may whisper and be whispered – the non-human body yearning.

References

Deleuze, G. and Guattari, F. (2004). *A Thousand Plateaus: Capitalism and Schizophrenia*. London : Continuum.

Deleuze, G. and Guattari, F. (1994). *What Is Philosophy?* London: Verso.

Paugam, C. (2015). Attempting the Embrace N° 22, [online] *Claire Paugam*. Available at: http://www.clairepaugam.com/Attempting-the-Embrace-n-22-1 [Accessed 4 Mar. 2017].

Paugam, C. (2014-2017). Attempting the Embrace. [videos, photographs, living matter installations, ceramics: online]. Available at: http://www.clairepaugam.com/ [Accessed 4 Mar. 2017].

Pignarre, P. and Stengers, I. (2011). *Capitalist Sorcery: Breaking the Spell*. Translated by Andrew Goffey. New York: Palgrave Macmillan.

Stafford, B. (2001). *Visual Analogy: Consciousness as the Art of Connecting*. Cambridge: MIT Press.

Stengers, I. and Despret, V. (2014). *Women Who Make a Fuss: The Unfaithful Daughters of Virginia Woolf*. Translated by April Knutson. 1st ed. Minneapolis, MN: Univocal Publishing.

Stengers, I. (2013). Introductory Notes on an Ecology of Practices. *Cultural Studies Review*, 11 (1), p. 183-196.

Amr Mosque in Cairo by Night
Effeietsanders, 2008

Extraordinary Happenings and Ordinary Affects

~~~~

Sabrina Lilleby
UNIVERSITY OF TEXAS AT AUSTIN

This project was undertaken during a period of excessive violence. A few years earlier, many citizens of Cairo considered artefacts of war such as tanks, machine guns, barbed wire and sandbags as belonging to a war-zone, not to their intimate cityscape. Yet, with the events that unraveled in the spring of 2011, dwellers of Cairo were tossed into a whirlwind of immediate experiences with the artefacts and acts of war. The previously mentioned items, together with explosions, check points and death sentences have now become part and parcel of the everyday for a majority of the population. Dwellers of this colossus of a city to often oscillate between glimpsing shimmers of alternative futures, and staring down dark ravines of hopelessness. However, between these intense outliers, the ordinary seem to carry on. In this paper, I suggest that although Cairenes increasingly encounter a number of extraordinary and violent events in their everyday life, these events get weaved in the fabric of everyday life and produce ordinary affects. My argument is not about apathy, nor of despair; it is not an exotic account of the other, or a subaltern tale of agency amidst misery. Instead, it is an account of the affects that circulate in an everyday that must carry on. To relay the affective, ephemeral, yet ordinary in contemporary Cairo, my paper— much inspired by Stewart (2007)— starts off with a short introduction, then recounts several short fragments. These snippets are based on number of personal experiences and stories collected in Cairo over the last five years.

KEYWORDS
Affect, Cairo, Everyday, The Urban, Violence

I.

A winter morning, a man far away from our city searched in the back of the cabinet for some matches. Then, he lit himself on fire. They say that is when it started – this period of excessive violence. The extensive list of characteristics of living in an authoritarian regime and in a neoliberal economy daily grows longer, as the dwellers of this colossus of a city we call Cairo oscillate between glimpsing alternative futures, and staring down gorges of hopelessness. Yet, between these outliers, the ordinary carries on. In the everyday, they encounter a number of extraordinary and violent events and objects, but these get woven into the fabric of everyday life and produce ordinary affects (Stewart 2007). The sort of experiences and moods I have been trying to grapple with recently occur here, in the middle between extraordinary events and objects and ordinary affects. But, how do we write this complex and concatenated world where nothing has yet to be coalesced?

When speaking of present Cairo, we could talk of the affective modes of fear; how fear leaks into the everyday. We could talk about how fear emanates from television screens; how it creeps across the living room floor and hits bodies, seeps in and fills that void where a sense of belonging used to dwell. But, this experience is daily nourished through media representations. Instead, this is an attempt to capture something more fleeting. What happens when people do not get scared, or when fear mixes with anger, happiness or lust? How do we capture that which did not happen or that which is yet to occur? This paper is not a paper about apathy, psychological repression or of despair; it is not an exotic account of the other or a subaltern tale of agency amidst misery. Instead, it is an account of the affects that circulate in everyday, a meditation on how we live in the suspense between the ordinary and extraordinary. Instead of rendering the city as inexplicable because of this seeming contradiction, I try to hold it in tension and write it. Consequently, this is not a conventional argument, it is an experiment in thought as well as in practice; the practice of writing the sensory topography of a city.

A few years ago, despite living with a despot, many dwellers of Cairo considered artifacts such as tanks, machine guns, barbed wire and sandbags as belonging to a war-zone, not to their intimate milieu. Yet, with the events that unraveled in the spring of 2011, dwellers of Cairo were tossed into a perplexing everyday where they have gained immediate experience with the objects and acts one supposed belonged to warfare. However, instead of being brought to a standstill, halted by fear, the city trudges on and the previously mentioned items, together with explosions, check points, brick walls, balaclava clad soldiers and executions have become part and parcel of the everyday. These items mix with the mundane tasks of cooking, chatting, singing, drinking, eating, fucking and crying. In subsuming these novel objects, the cadence and pulse of the ordinary skips a beat and then returns to its rhythmic beat. What happens when people are not unnerved; when the extraordinary becomes the ordinary, or when panic mixes with anger, happiness or lust? Something happens, but it cannot be properly named. It hits us more like a mood, a pressure in the atmosphere or reverberations in the ambience (Brennan 2004). In what follows below I try to relay happenings, experiences, moods and subjects before they have yet to be properly named. This is me trying to comprehend a city but also an acknowledgement that it cannot ever really be grasped.

Cairo as a space in this text takes the shape of a series of instances, stories and encounters collected from my own and my interlocutors' everyday lives over the last five years. These are mixed with references to news pieces as well as rumors or urban myths I heard often while waiting for the metro, in taxis, waiting for meetings, waiting for the doctor, waiting for the man with the stamp to return from prayer or waiting for the afternoon traffic to unknot itself. These notes are mixed with conversations I had with acquaintances and friends about one particular but extensive topic. During these talks I would offer the theme of the intermingling between the mundane and extraordinary in everyday life in Cairo. I would ask what sort of feelings, happenings, episodes and memories would offer themselves up. If I had chosen to use names when referring to my interlocutors, these would undeniably have had to be changed for security reasons. However, I opted out of using names altogether in order to relay a sense of a shared experience of the present. Stories can both be owned and shared. Anecdotes circulating in the city show how these often take on a life of their own.

Apart from the absurdity of the everyday, the themes of circulation, transmission, and movement most often turned into repeated refrains during these conversations. Much like the city's traffic, my co-conversationalists would speak of being in perpetual motion not necessarily in order to represent or to understand but merely to make ends meet. They would speak of movement without a particular goal, but still movement as an embodied everyday practice. They would speak of a life haunted by the memory of major social uprisings occurring as if out of nowhere, perhaps merely because bodies aligned themselves in productive constellations at the correct time: a shopkeeper on fire in Tunis, a young man found tortured to death at a police station in Alexandria, a son being groomed for taking over the presidential palace, and hundreds of sleeping strikers dotting the sidewalks of Kasr el Aini. Bodies that meet in the social, produce reverberations, affects and allies (Butler 2011). It is hard to forget or suppress that possibilities rest in their meeting, in the feeling of bumping up against each other, and the subsequent doing and acting, the touching, affecting and reshuffling (Spinoza 2002).

Daily, human life in Cairo, just like hard currency, seems to diminish in value. Then, what remains? Where do we go from here? This text provides no blueprint but the last few lines I offer up near the end gesture towards the inherent possibilities of movement as being. An inkling and hunch, nudging and whispering that potential rests somewhere in the future present (Bergson 2001). A precarious life seems to me a life fated to perpetual motion marked by continual uncertainty. As a response, we can resign in despair since this is a life other than promised by multiple modernist political projects or we can take a deep breath and look around (Tsing 2015). In a world where all we know is that we have to get up in the morning, to trudge on in a silence imposed by excessive external violence and internal apathy, the city might seem silent. However, before I move on to the next section I want to re-assert that it is precisely in the act of getting up in the morning, and the subsequent movement, where possibilities of new constellations, alignments and alliances lay.

II.

She was in a meditation class because Cairo is just the kind of city where meditation becomes appealing and necessary. During the break she couldn't reach him and thought of how he entered the apartment the day before. How he had run to the bathroom vomiting from all the teargas, heaving for his breath. The thoughts kept on seeping into her mind between the exhalations and inhalations. Breathe in. Breathe out. She checked her phone again. A message from him that read "hey can we skype. my phone is dead... by the way i got shot but i'm doing fine." On Skype, she sees that his face is distorted from one of the thirty pellets that had permeated his body. His mom appears on the screen. She is making him tea and gathering the laundry.

One day, two years later, she walks down the same street where he was shot. A graffiti artist has painted a large mural on a wall. It depicts an enormous lifelike heart on a blood-red and orange background, and a speech bobble that states, "hope". Someone else has hurriedly written in answer, "fuck you and fuck your hope— we are living in a counter-revolution". The state has set up traffic lights on that street. Waiting at the red light, pedestrians and drivers alike move through a gallery of murals memorializing the bloodshed from two years past.

Around the same time as he got shot, young cosmopolitan Cairenes met on a beach in the very south of Egypt to dance and drink— a sort of Egyptian Woodstock if you will. This year, the organizers decided it was too dangerous to have the festival on an open beach and chose to move it to one of the gated resorts up the coast. She and her husband were now sitting in their bedroom talking about the festival. They were mocking the cowardly upper class youth that didn't dare to move out of their comfort zone. Then, they heard the boom and felt the shock; the windows reverberated from the tremor of the bomb. Fear filled her as she called her friend who was walking her dog. No, not to worry, she said. Apparently it was just a bomb at the church two streets down and nobody had gotten hurt.

Nobody knew who put it there. But again, that was also before some young techie developed an app that could tell the location of bombs around town. She avoided the metro that day and got in a cab to go to her weekly writing group. They had started without her. One of the group members was from Beirut, and had already lived through two civil wars— she smiled understandingly and continued sharing her text with the group.

She had been walking her dog with another Lebanese friend a few weeks earlier. As they strolled through an empty desert valley just outside of Cairo, with the little white and fluffy dog playing among the rocks, they heard the sound of military aircrafts sear through the sky. Her friend gasped in fear. It reminded her of a dream from the night before, itself an echo of a real life nightmare twenty years earlier. She told her friend about one night when she was eight. She had asked her mom, "What is that sound?" and her mom answered, "Hush, keep practicing for your math test." The next morning, she passed her math exam with excellence; but over thirty people had died from the bombs the night before. Temporarily drawn lines between past and present, and, between childhood and adulthood blur. The celebration of life intermingles with the mourning of the dead.

After visiting a friend who had just given birth, she walked down the street of a posh neighborhood when she saw the beautiful flowers between two embassy buildings. The man selling the flowers was wearing a long traditional garb and would not have fit into the sumptuous neighborhood had it not been for the inexpensive, yet exquisite, flowers he was selling. Suddenly she heard one of the soldiers guarding an embassy yelling, "run, run". She catches the sound of an empty machine gun going off. Tac tac. Some soldiers run. She is filled with terror and wants to run, but calls, "What? What is that?" to the old man selling flowers. He responds, "no problem, no problem," but she starts moving fast in the opposite direction. Then the soldiers all start laughing. It is a game. They were bored.

Boredom is all too familiar to anyone living in a megapolis. Everyone and their grandmother spend hours commuting in the overcrowded traffic. Someone tells her about their bus ride home from work. Halfway home, the bus came to a stop. The passengers, tired from a long day of labor and eager to return home for dinner, looked up annoyed as the bus came to a halt. Terrified faces attached to rapidly moving bodies started running from the large stadium towards the bus. But the vehicle moved on. The workers had to get home for dinner. Later, they read in the newspaper that some of the commuters had not gone home for dinner. Instead, they had gotten out of their car and beat up one of the fleeing football fans in true vigilante fashion. The people, and that thing we call the state, merge in the social life of Cairo. And since the army officially took over, its chorus has been the constant repetition of two words, "Terror and Security, Security and Terror."

Strangely though, statistics show that the most dangerous everyday activity is crossing the street. You regularly observe individuals driving down the wrong lane on the highway dauntingly facing the ongoing traffic. Their kid is hanging out of the window, sucking in the wind, while they listen to the hourly news broadcast announcing that the latest patriarch has declared a state of emergency. The driver and his kid feel comforted. They can get home before the rush hour begins.

Sometimes that which we want the most is what actually creates the opposite. Not only does the attempt to make everything coherent impede our actual understanding, but our quest for security leads to insecurity. A sudden surge occurs in the incarceration of protesters, gays, communists, islamists, terrorists, doctors, professors, poets and NGO workers. Simultaneously, jokes are produced at an intensive speed. The state, its oppression, and the reactions to it, provides enough material for a proverbial fountain of jokes. One day, some of the hordes of political prisoners were finally released on bail. But, it was not only prisoners who came out of the prison gates. Together with the detainees came a flock of ostriches. Rumor has it that you can only be served ostrich eggs at upscale hotels dotting the banks of the Nile — the Mariott, the Hilton, the Four Seasons, the Hyatt Regency— but apparently you can breed them in jail.

CAPACIOUS

You can incarcerate a person – even an ostrich – but you cannot incarcerate a joke. A joke might surface amidst a crammed group of passengers stuck in a minivan during a traffic jam, but it travels faster than the small white buses dotting the highway. It rolls down the street like an avalanche taking down everyone in its path. It lays bare the ridiculousness and absurdity of imminent precarity in the same way as cries from protesters who confront power and capital. But that was before they went to jail.

Somehow it has been forgotten that initially people were rioting about the lack of bread and the lack of healthcare. This goal is only recalled in rare glimpses. Such a glimpse occurred when they went to the fancy private hospital to do a biopsy, and gave the doctor his money in a white, unmarked envelope over the surgery table. Kidneys are traded like fresh beans at the market; like pellets from a rifle. While among those who used to protest, casings from the pellets become memorabilia— a nostalgia of the time they still dared to take to the street to protest the fact that some people cannot own their own kidneys. Sometimes the bullet hits, sometimes it does not reach the target.

It is an ardent task tracing the lines of flight of bodies that meet in the social. More often than we would like to admit, happenings can be attributed to mere chance. The image that spurred the affective avalanche that was to come, was of a man hundreds of kilometers away who was driven to the edge of sanity and lit himself on fire. Or, was he the mad one? When your entire social world seemingly pretends like nothing even happened, or is happening - getting out the matchbox does seem mundane, yet powerfully lucid.

Those with a penchant for psychoanalysis like to attribute madness to the suffering of the past, but what about the trauma of the present? In Cairo's alternative health centers who cater to thick wallets, practitioners speak about the important link between diet and mental health. They do not speak about how the lack of a diet, and the daily struggle for food affects one's sanity.

Yet, although madness becomes ordinary, the city is suspended in perpetual motion, moving around, making ends meet. Life does not stop because it cannot stop. The labor of worlding trudges on. The new minister of justice told us that," We are the masters and the rest are the slaves", but a cabdriver says, "They don't know our anger, no one can tell the future except God".

The multitudes oscillate between motion and rest. Sometimes the motion accelerates and comes to exceed that which was previously imagined. The unthought-of and unspoken gets articulated. Masses of singularities transform into a dangerous wave— a maelstrom of affinity that can only be intersected by a red wave. Then, they are slaughtered by the hundreds.

He was working as a video journalist at the time of the massacre, and his boss had sent him to the large mosque where they kept the bodies, to videotape the scene. On the steps of the mosque— turned morgue— hundreds of people had crowded together pushing towards the doors of god's house. The smell of the sweat from victims' family members mixed with the odors of journalists and other voyeurs. It was perhaps even worse than the smell of the 700 bodies on the floor inside. Without luck, he pushed and he pushed to get inside to capture those bodies on two minutes of film in order to keep his job. Then a new group of mourners arrived, carrying yet another dead body, and the doors of the building shot open. He grabbed on to the side of the body, starting to carry it— his role in the scene seemingly changing from journalist to mourner. When he came inside, he looked around. The mass of dead bodies moved him into silence. He captured the scene on camera, but it took six more months before he would speak of that unspeakable scene.

After the massacre, they fought over being the divine's mouthpiece on this plane of existence. In numerous apartments around the city, humans cohabitate with the jinn. When an otherworldly creature refuses to acknowledge that the curtain between our world and their world should remain closed, you call the priest or the sheikh who will exorcise the specter. If they cannot come, you play religious CDs of holy texts. A jinn is real, but 700 dead bodies, 700 entire life stories, fall prey to collective amnesia. But, in our world not only humans are actors. Absence, or utter silence itself, becomes the strongest actor of all. It simmers and reverberates under our streets, under our skin, in our guts, until one day it bursts, and the silence becomes so loud that it turns to noise. And another man searches in the back of the cabinet for the matches and lights himself on fire. His image affects us, and once again, the silence is broken.

References

Agamben, G. (1998). Homo Sacer: Sovereign Power and Bare Life. Stanford: Stanford University Press.

Amar, P. (2006). Cairo Cosmopolitan: Politics, Culture, and Urban Space in the New Globalized Middle East. Cairo: American University in Cairo Press.

Bergson, H. (2001). Time and Free Will: An Essay on the Immediate Data of Consciousness. Mineola, N.Y: Dover Publications.

Berlant, L. (2011). Cruel Optimism. Durham & London: Duke University Press.

Brennan, T. (2014). The Transmission of Affect. Ithaca & London: Cornell University Press.

Butler, J. (2011). Bodies in Alliance and the Politics of the Street. Lecture.

Casarino, C. (2011). Marx before Spinoza: Notes toward an Investigation. In: D. Vardoulakis, ed., Spinoza Now, 1st ed. London: University of Minnesota Press, pp.179–236.

Certeau, M. de. (2011). The Practice of Everyday Life. Oakland: University of California Press.

Das, V. (2007). Life and Words: Violence and the Descent Into the Ordinary. Oakland: University of California Press.

Deleuze, G. and Guattari, F. (2001). Thousand Plateaus. London & New York: Continuum.

Elyachar, J. (2010). Phatic labor, infrastructure, and the question of empowerment in Cairo. American Ethnologist, 37 (3), pp.452–464.

Foucault, M. (1997). Ethics: Subjectivity and Truth. New York: New Press.

Latour, B. (2007). Reassembling the Social: An Introduction to Actor-Network-Theory. Oxford: Oxford University Press.

Law, J. (2004). After Method: Mess in Social Science Research. New York & London: Routledge.

Marx, K. (1994). The Eighteenth Brumaire of Louis Bonaparte. New York: International Publishers.

Navaro-Yashin, Y. (2002). Faces of the State: Secularism and Public Life in Turkey. Princeton: Princeton University Press.

Papadopoulos, D., Stephenson, N. and Tsianos, V. (2008). Escape routes: control and subversion in the twenty-first century. London & Ann Arbor: Pluto Press.

Seigworth, G.J. and Gregg, M. (2010). An Inventory of Shimmers. In: The Affect Theory Reader. Gregg, M. and Seigworth, G.J ed, 1st ed. Durham & London: Duke University Press, pp.1–29.

Spinoza, B (2002). The Ethics. In: The Complete Works. Shirley, S. and Morgan, M.L., ed. 1st ed. Indianapolis: Hackett Publishing, pp.213–382.

Stewart, K. (2007). Ordinary Affects. Durham & London: Duke University Press.

Stewart, K. (2010). Worlding Refrains. In: M. Gregg and G.J. Seigworth, eds. The Affect Theory Reader, 1st ed. Durham & London: Duke University Press, pp.339–355.

Tsing, A.L. (2015). The Mushroom at the End of the World: On the Possibility of Life in Capitalist Ruins. Princeton: Princeton University Press.

Feeling Poetry

Mercy Romero
SONOMA STATE UNIVERSITY

At the graduation ceremony I sit with some of the other women of color who teach in the school of Arts and Humanities. There are a handful of us amongst the few rows of faculty seated on stage. Friends and family of the graduates sit in the stacked wooden balconies that circle the stage like a rib cage. The back doors of the hall are opened onto an expanse of green lawn, where an overflow of guests gathers to view the ceremony from afar, and if they choose, via a jumbo TV.

My nephew is walking today. That I can sit just one row back on the stage he'll cross to receive his diploma feels like a gift not a workday, although it is this too. His family is here. My daughter is somewhere out on the lawn with all the other family members. I feel humbled that she can see me at work, funny that I am robed and sat up high. She runs around the campus greens with her little cousins. Her open run and play too might signal a kind of place-making practice.

I was in middle school when I first set foot on a college campus, a participant in a summer program called PRIME (Philadelphia Region Introduction for Minorities to Engineering). The program was mostly for Philly kids, but it bussed a bunch of us from Camden, New Jersey into the city just across the bridge. We were encouraged to think about possible futures in science and math, but more so it brought us all together, and made the university a place that might be possible for us, kids of color from working poor families doing an accelerated course of math in a different university classroom from 6th-11th grade. It is probably why I chose to stay the academic route and try to become a professor: the fun of those hot Julys spent studying at a university campus with my peers from all over the region. I still have some of my ID cards tucked away in a drawer with a few childhood things, the ones from Drexel and Penn. Eventually I took a turn into the humanities. When I was just about 16 years old, Black poetry gave me the language to hold and name my life: "traveling. i'm / always traveling" (Sanchez, 1985). Called me into perspective, thought, language, and love. This is still the case for me.

The Arts and Humanities graduation program features readings by two women poets, an English professor and a graduating senior. Dee Dee Simpson is one of the few Black students who will walk the stage today. That she will also read a poem, the condensed beauty of the word, is part of what makes the ceremony for me. A pressed little bob sits on her head in place of a graduation cap. I didn't wear my cap either, and instead pull my hair into a low-slung bun. Another Black professor and I talk about this as we prepare to walk out. She forgoes her cap too. It feels like we are going a bit rogue, disjointing our regalia.

Simpson shies at the podium and her fellow graduating seniors call out and begin to clap, signs that she is among friends and it is all good to begin. With this, we are probably a majority poised in our seats for her reading. Some part of ceremony has this other set of feelings running through, the beauty in becoming vulnerable and then the rest of the folks gathered who are in it with you, tell you that you are going to be okay, hold the space, just come on through.

The poem she delivers explores being Black in the United States given its constitutive anti-Blackness, the 2016 election of Donald Trump, and the beginnings of mass protests against his presidency. In the poem she says that her feelings have not changed, and tells liberal minded white people that she will not pretend to be outraged or participate in a legible protest, because let's face it, Black people needed your solidarity and assembly for a long time now, and you failed to show up, *en masse*. Yet saying this is also the reach out, that constant work. Early on in her reading of her poem, and as if setting a small fire, she says the word fuck.

Her poem makes me think about home. She takes us to the outskirts of her neighborhood, a place she says you would not come to, even if you were riding in an armored truck. I think about what it means to be able to hold onto (keep) your cultural traditions and things, at and against a traumatic legacy of coloniality, deportation and internment, the theft of property and land, and the ensuing racial violation of the right-less and un/propertied. Black studies scholar George Lipsitz's discusses the Black spatial imaginary, those affirming cultural practices that stretch against the housing and police violence of white supremacy's hyper segregation, and invite Black life. I wonder where she is from, and hold that thought with where I am from too, what it means to grow in the wake of all this, and hone the vastness of our imaginations, music, and poetries together (Sharpe, 2016). Her poetry gets to it, the vexed socialities, the documentation of these (ongoing) legacies of racial terror and dispossession.

Can our collective listening and thinking fill up this orchestra hall? It was designed to hold classical concerts. It is described as a world-class hall in terms of its acoustical design. But it isn't the best place to listen to the poet who is standing at a mike with her back to you. Sometimes the sound rises up and is lost to you. So you look past all the black robes, what might pass as sameness, take in the rows of graduating seniors in their decorated caps, sandals, heels, stilettos, dresses, shorts and shades, all the energy gone into making them stand out just a bit this day. At the close of her poem there is admiration, cheering, and clapping, and she turns to head back to her seat just next to the faculty member poet. I watch her sit and wonder at her courage. She is visibly relieved when she leans into the camaraderie of the other poet who grasps and holds her forearm.

I try to snap a picture of my nephew as he crosses the stage in his black robe and neon green frat sash to receive his diploma, but I'm too nervous to get up or hold my phone up too high, so I miss the shot. The colleagues I am sitting with said I should have told them, because they might have tried too. My nephew is one of just four or five Black male students who will walk in this ceremony.

After the ceremony my daughter runs over to me looking hot and sly and she greets me:

    - Did you like the poem Mami, the Black girl's poem?
    - Yes, my love. I liked it very much.
    - Did you hear what she said?

My daughter is trying to indicate to me that the poet used the word fuck. I can't recall if she repeats the cuss or not. Many people are gathering in the vestibule. This cuss will become a sticking point later, what the poem will teach children to say (think?) and the idea of what is appropriate and parental offense.

I tell her it's the right word to use sometimes. You need to figure that out in poetry. I'm not sure if she hears me either, but I know she's taking it all in. Together, and given the beauty of the day we are each overjoyed that these two things have come together: an opportunity to understand that poetry is precise and worldly, and that another Black girl has been held and represented at the mike.

Some days later fragments of the poem surface in spectacular media headlines. A few emails take offense with its "use" of politics and profanity. Reports of an informal and private administrative apology reinscribe liberal family values, propriety, and enjoyment. The assurance given is had the content of the poem been known (read) before, it would have never seen the light of the ceremony. Although thousands do not object, the poem is herein strangely and symbolically cancelled, as if it's reading could be retroactively undone, marked and remembered as a mistake.[1] The faculty poet who also read that day (her poem takes me to a pond with a partial view of late spring and my own fading calla lilies) was quoted in the newspaper as saying that the graduating poet's performance evoked strong response because it "was good work." Invocations of ceremony may mean there is going to be some work going on. If ceremony gathers and works today, there may be some kind of revelation at our converging experiences of the long histories of racial terror, particularly for members of the university community who have been made to live and teach through this everyday violence (Clifton, 1991).

No YouTube recordings of Dee Dee Simpson's reading surface. She refuses media requests for interviews and has yet to publish the text of her poem. We can understand her refusal as a refusal of racial terror, another kind of protest. Black protest is in the interest of protection. Protection of kinship and community, body and mind. Just a few days earlier, Princeton University professor, Keeanga-Yamahtta Taylor's graduation speech at Hampshire College is recorded and circulated, and she begins to receive death threats. Like Simpson, Taylor refuses racial terror, refuses to appear there and keeps her practice instead focused at the creative insight and futurity of dissent.

The first time I participated in an arts integration effort on campus I took my students to an evening play. We viewed a student production of "The Hummingbird Wars." Afterwards I was full of the play, the beauty of student performance, and the total mix-up and alienation of life, which the play explodes. My partner and our kids decided to play video games and then come pick me up after the play. It was about 9 p.m. On our way off campus we were pulled over by a campus police officer. Although I wasn't driving, the officer asked what I was doing on campus. I responded I had gone to see a play. He asked me if I was a student. I said no. I am a professor. He asked me for my faculty ID. I said no (our ID doesn't actually specify our jobs). Why was he asking me for ID? Instead, I asked him for his name and told him I would be contacting his supervisor. All the while and running behind my voice I was thinking about Sandra Bland, as I had been for weeks. I felt a kinship with her. The officer had his gun on his hip and I wanted him to get the fuck away from us, from my children who were wilting in the back seat. I was thinking about how he had a gun that close to my son and my daughter; I had labored to get them each into this world. The children I had nursed for four years each. I thought about the violence of guns, how that threat had shaped my childhood. The mother in me wanted to grab his gun and throw it into the bushes.

In a meeting with his supervisor a week later I was casually informed that the reason the officer would have asked me as a passenger for my ID (my complaint to his supervisor) would have been because he thought that I was a prostitute.

There were so few Black students at graduation. So few Black families and friends gathered on the green expanse or in the music hall. So few Black faculty members. The poem extends and contracts here, at what passes as the everyday and into the deeper feelings of a ceremony. If I had a solo I might scream

> a fair use of that particular sound space, designed for the shriek and shrill of stringed instruments,
>
> that orchestration.

References

Clifton, L. (1991) "won't you celebrate with me" from *The Collected Poems of Lucille Clifton*. 1965-2010, BOA Editions, Ltd.

Lipsitz, G. (2011). *How Racism Takes Place*, Philadelphia: Temple University Press.

Payne, P. (2017) "Critics blast SSU graduation poem as 'hate speech,'" The Press Democrat, May 24. http://www.pressdemocrat.com/news/7024591-181/critics-blast-ssu-graduation-poem

Sanchez, S. (1999). "Poem at thirty" from *Shake Loose My Skin: New and Collected Poems*, Boston: Beacon Press.

Sharpe, C. (2017) *In the Wake: On Blackness and Being*, Durham: Duke University Press.

Endnotes

1. In response to reports of an informal university apology, a petition signed by faculty, staff, alumni, and concerned community members is delivered to the university administration in support of the poem, and to encourage dialogue and dissent from what is imagined as a singular response.

Cover, *San-Chōme no Yūhi (Vol 8.): Yūyake no Uta*
Ryōhei Saigan, 1979

On Manga, Mimetics and the Feeling of (Reading a) Language

Toward a Situated Translational Practice

~~~~~

Gretchen Jude
UNIVERSITY OF CALIFORNIA DAVIS

Graphic novels, by combining images with printed words, engage readers in narrative experiences comparable to the immersive quality of cinema. The rich tradition of manga, Japan's venerable and wide-ranging graphic narrative form, employs an array of graphical and linguistic strategies to engage readers, bodily as well as mentally and emotionally. Among these strategies, Japanese mimetics: a grammatical class of sound words, work effectively to transmit aural, tactile, and proprioceptive states. Yet most Japanese mimetics have no English equivalent and can only be expressed with phrase-length explanations or glosses; the somatic nature of mimetics thus resists translation. By grappling with the question of how to effectively express in English such translation-resistant linguistic forms, the author explores approaches to translation that attend to embodied and affective states such as those induced by mimetics. Experimental translational practices may thus attend to the affective and bodily-lived pressures felt when experiencing the in-between-ness of language(s). The structure of this paper accordingly follows the trajectory of a journey through (one reader's) translation and translational practice.

KEYWORDS

Nomadic Translation, Manga, Scanlation, Mimetics, Nostalgia

The Conditions of Translation: My Story

On the eve of my return to the U.S. after eight years in Tokyo, I went to a movie with my Japanese then-spouse. We both enjoyed the light nostalgic tone of "ALWAYS *Sanchōme no Yūhi*" [*Always: Sunset on Third Street*]. Even more, I felt satisfied with how much of the dialogue I had been able to understand. I picked up the print version of the story right away; the movie, I was pleased to discover, was based on a long-running *manga* series. In the decade since my relocation back to my home country, Ryōhei Saigan's *Sanchōme no Yūhi* has become a mainstay of my Japanese language practice.

Raised speaking Standard American English, I have never felt comfortable claiming to 'know' Japanese. Despite years of study and positive interactions, I remain insecure about my linguistic fluency—one look at a Japanese newspaper reminds me of how much I still don't (and may never) know. I am also conscious of how my own status as a white person comes up against Japanese national-racial identity constructions. In any given context, I am reminded that I am definitely 'not Japanese' even when Japanese friends kindly compliment me by calling me 'more Japanese than' themselves.

On the other hand, living and working with Japanese people in Japanese contexts for nearly a decade changed me irrevocably. Inasmuch as I 'know Japanese'–by which I mean, I can function in Japanese-language contexts–I feel myself to be a different person than the one I was growing up in Idaho. These distinctions are distinctly felt ones, as I physically behave differently depending on the context. Outside Japan, opening *Sanchōme no Yūhi* causes echoes of these physical states to resound through me.

When I read, I feel simultaneously both aware of my own activity of reading a 'foreign' language and swept up in the enjoyment of being able to stand in as the text's (passing-as-Japanese) addressee. The pleasure of understanding is complexly kinesthetic and emotional, evoking not only awareness of the narrative progression but also of sounds (of a train echoing through the city, of noisy summer-night insects), smells (of smoking chicken fat), sensations (of humid night air, of feet numb from sitting *seiza* on *tatami*) and emotions (closeness, nostalgia, longing, and loss). What often surprises me is how intense my emotions can be when I encounter such texts in Japanese, especially since I am usually so resistant to these feelings when I engage with American mass media objects.

CAPACIOUS

From these embodied experiences, questions arise: how does the text continue to perform its effects on me, yet again reinscribing my relationship to Japaneseness (and all the places and people this signifies for me personally)? Indeed, how does a text *'make* me feel'? How to make the relevance of these feelings, relationships and experiences clear in the cross-linguistic texts I produce? In short, I wish to interrogate the ways in which my interlanguage experience is a firmly embodied one.

In this paper, I will explore how the manga form uses linguistic, narrative, and graphic strategies to evoke embodied reactions in readers. Translations of manga (and other Japanese texts) can be produced and received in ways that may potentially problematize and complicate schemas of national-cultural identity. I will examine one such practice, that of scanlation. Scanlators' communal, virtual sites of translation provide examples of a postmodern translational practice that stems from a different conceptualization of the modern (individual) translating subject. Finally, I will suggest alternatives to models of translation based on and reifying the national-cultural subject, alternatives based on Sakai's notion of *subject in transit* (2006) and Braidotti's idea of the *nomadic* subject (2011). While my approach may be untenable for professional translators working in institutional contexts, this paper aims to suggest new sites and strategies for creative/imaginative work that may facilitate the next step into an as-yet-unimagined as-yet-unimagined future of translation.

Making A Manga's Story Mine

Ryōhei Saigan's work of short graphic fiction "*Otsukimi no Yoru*" ["*Harvest Moon*", lit. "Moon-viewing Evening"] revolves around young salaryman Yusuke Machida's encounter with audible yet unseen animals called *tanuki*. Puzzlingly called 'raccoon-dogs' in English, *tanuki* have a long association with Japanese folklore; Saigan here embeds their imputed magical powers in a story of loss and longing. The first half of the story portrays idealized middle-class urban life in the heady years of Japan's post-war recovery; the central conflict lies between the pressure to work, symbolized by the boss' expectation that Machida will spend his afterwork time playing *settai gorufu* (golf games set up for entertaining clients), and Machida's desire to enjoy some time with his family, in this case an evening of *otsukimi* (moon-viewing with food, drink, and socializing). The ironic pivot of this conflict is encapsulated in the term *kazoku sābisu*, which combines the Sino-Japanese word for 'family' (*kazoku*) with the more recent loan from English 'service' (*sābisu*). The Japanese businessman of this period was expected to support his family by working extremely long hours; *kazoku sābisu* turns these expectations around to include support of the family by (at least occasionally) being present with them.

Machida drunk at the yakitori shop, *Otsukimi no Yoru*, Ryōhei Saigan, 2005

Another pivotal term in the narrative is *yakitori* (charcoal-grilled chicken on skewers). This tasty, casual dish is Machida's son Yūtaro's favorite. In the course of the story, Machida encounters the *yakitori* shop owner twice; both times, this denizen of *shitamachi* (Tokyo's working class neighborhood) is the purveyor of key information. During their first meeting, he points out to Machida, and the reader, that the *tanuki* will surely be out in the green empty lots nearby, since there is a bright full moon. And in fact, as Machida walks home through this liminal urban space, the iconic sound of the *tanuki* drumming on their bellies rises up out of the chorus of summer insects. The happy scene is rounded out with Machida opening the door to his happy family, with whom he shares a lovely evening. These frames (in which there is no dialogue) exemplify the happy home of this time, with the symmetrical domestic space framed by the abundance of late-summer fruit, rice cakes and flowers; however, next to this image is a cinematic reverse-cut to the same abundance looking out over the moon shining on the noisy urban wilderness. The sound of the family laughing is juxaposed with the sound of insects and the *tanuki*, foreshadowing the turn in the narrative.

A sense of domestic bliss, *Otsukimi no Yoru*, Ryōhei Saigan, 2005

In fact, the reversal is complete and devastating, as a disoriented Machida is awakened from his dream of domestic bliss by a kind police officer, only to find his *yakitori* devoured and his home a lonely mess. At last he remembers, his family had been killed in an accident the year before, and his vision of domestic bliss, only a memory. The denouement finds Machida once again at the *yakitori* shop, this time sad and drunk; the similarity of his conversation with the shop owner only underlines the tragic difference in this scene. The shop owner explains the situation to another customer, filling in the details of Machida's tragically empty life. In the final scene, we find Machida again on the path through the abandoned lot, pleading with the (still-unseen) *tanuki* to once again take him back into his dream of the past; they remain silent, however, as an image of his wife and son appear in the moon. His tears remain as the pair happily exhort him to resume his ordinary life, yet, as their image fades, he smiles through the tears. In the last frame, the *tanuki* drumming sounds resume and Machida stands alone on the cusp of an unknown future.

The bittersweetness of this particular storyline, while one of the more tragic, reflects the nostalgic timbre of the manga series, *Sanchōme no Yūhi*, as a whole. Ryōhei Saigan's award-winning series first saw publication in 1974, portraying working-class Tokyo circa 1955-1970, and as of 2013, 60 volumes have been published. In addition, stories from the series have been adapted as a TV *anime* series (1990-1991), and a trilogy of feature films, the first of which won a Japanese Academy Award in 2005 (*Wikipedia*).

Many of the reasons behind its popularity with general audiences in Japan are also reasons why it has not been among the many works exported for English-speaking audiences (Douglass et al 2011). Not only are many themes and underlying cultural assumptions difficult to translate, the premise and function of the series rely heavily on the evocation of nostalgia. As Ivy (1995) points out, nostalgia for an idealized pre-modern Japan is inextricably linked with the on-going construction of (post)modern Japanese identity. This feeling of nostalgia is actually a desire for something that never existed, yet it is imbricated in the ongoing construction of the Japanese national subject, since under this schema "what makes the Japanese so different from everyone else makes them identical to each other" (Ivy 1995, 9). Interestingly, even the much more recent past can also be subject to this process; perhaps in the case of Tokyo, the very rapidity of its, literally physical and seemingly perpetual, reconstruction makes it an excellent candidate for ongoing projects of representation as a 'lost' past and object of nostalgia.

Saigan's stories of Japan before the Bubble Economy hinge on the pleasure of imaginatively inhabiting a past that did not necessarily exist in the reader's own experience. This process, which relies on a feeling of lack, is also a material and embodied one: "The vanishing, which (dis)embodies in its gerund form the movement of something passing away, gone but not quite, suspended between presence and absence, located at a point that both is and is not here in the repetitive process of absenting" (Ivy 1995, 20). Stories about the 1950s that Saigan began to tell in the 1970s, riding the wave of the massive economic boom that has literally transformed the Tokyo landscape, continue still to rework the pre-Bubble past, making it a vanishing point for readers to temporarily (re)inhabit that collective imaginary. Like Machida in his domestic dream, the reader may be transported 'back in time' by Saigan as the trickster-manga author. The *tanuki* themselves are doubly in Ivy's vanishing point: they are never seen, only heard. Their powers are palpable yet mysterious: did they eat the *yakitori* in return for inducing Machida's oneiric evening of family moon-viewing, or did Machida eat the kebabs himself in a drunken stupor? Their intentions remain similarly ambiguous: Machida's final offering to the *tanuki* is left unopened in his hands following his parting exchange with the apparitions of his loved ones, even as the *tanuki* drumming echoes in the distance. Furthermore, as both living mammals that still inhabit Japan's interstitial wilds and as long-standing icons of folk magic and superstition, the figure of the *tanuki* grounds constructions of ineffable nostalgia in ostensible reality.

The final Machida family reunion, *Otsukimi no Yoru*, Ryōhei Saigan, 2005

It is the imaginary artifice of Japanese nostalgia that makes it, somewhat ironically, also work on me as a queer white woman. For, while no construction of Japanese identity would count me as being legitimately 'Japanese,' even actual Japanese people feel nostalgia for their (essentialized) national past largely by participating in a complex system of linguistic and sensory projections existing in the present. That *manga*, cinema, TV, and other multisensory genres are ideal media for creating such feelings, and also account for my own feelings of nostalgia for/while inhabiting the world of *Sanchōme*: the part of me that acquired 'native-like' Japanese (along with a dozen years of embodied experiences and emotional commitments) is the part of me to which that nostalgia appeals.

The question remains as to how I might produce a translation that could have such effects on readers even further from Japan(eseness) than me. Is it desirable—or even possible—to mute the life experiences that were essential to my acquiring Japanese linguistic and cultural knowledge? Before exploring these questions, I will first address how the figure of translator is problematized by hybrid, multi-media texts such as *manga*.

In his *History of Translation: The Invisibility of the Translator*, Venuti distinguishes between two main approaches to translation, domesticating and foreignizing, both of which present the translator with ethical dilemmas. While a domesticating translation aims to draw the reader into intimate connection with the text, this approach enacts an ethnocentric erasure of cultural distance and difference. On the other hand, a foreignizing approach to translation, while leaving intact the values of the 'foreign' culture within the translated text (potentially enlarging the reader's worldview), also risks exoticizing and essentializing another's cultural practices. The horns of this dilemma have long defined Western translational theory. But what about literary works that do not rely solely on writing to convey meaning and aesthetic experience? How might multimedia works such as *manga* broaden our understanding—not only of what it means to translate, but also of what we do, and feel, when we encounter a textual narrative? How does the weaving of language, image, text, and context define the translational encounter? In looking for ways to navigate a translation of Saigan's "*Otsukimi no Yoru*" while neither domesticating nor exoticizing, I looked first to my predecessors, the scanlators.

Adventures in Manga Scanlation

Graphical narrative works in print, more than other written texts, are multi-sensory and experiential, relying on embodied participation of the reader to construct their meaning. Potsch and Williams (2012) characterize the genre of comics as "cinema without motion or sound" (13). They point out that American action comics use visual symbols, such as impact flashes, to show movement and force. Furthermore, these symbols generate embodied knowledge by referring to common image schemas, which are "derived from bodily experience in the physical world and conceptual metaphors linking different domains of experience. Thus, through ordinary processes of meaning construction, readers add time, motion, and event structure to the panels on the page" in order to generate meaning from the material provided by the author in print (34).

Implications for the translator of the performative, hybrid nature of graphical texts like manga are laid out by Rampant (2010) in his examination of the practice of scanlation. The very neologism (combining 'scan' and 'translation') makes clear the hybridity of the practice, which Douglass et al (2011) describe as "scanning original Japanese editions of manga, translating the text into another language, then using image-editing software to replace the Japanese…with the translation" (201). In addition, the singular figure of the translator, mirrored by the individual author of the original text, is replaced on both sides by collaborative groups of people spread over vast distances. While the manga itself is nominally authored and drawn by one main author, it is facilitated by numerous (usually unnamed) technicians in the publishing field–more so than typical print publications, given the multimediality of the form. Scanlation, an informal practice that arose among the spatially dispersed subculture of *shōnen manga* [manga for teen boys] fans, is an even more cooperative exercise. Scanlators work online in teams of "translators, editors, photomanipulators…, and scanners" (Rampant 2010, 226); some groups even commit to working after commercial translations are available from the publisher, incurring "'pirate status'" within their scanlation community (227).

Of course, the practice itself originated in the margins of a small subculture, as a reaction to a perceived lack of official translations of popular manga. Since the 1990s, the scanlation community has grown so influential that, as Rampant claims, "translational norms [of *shōnen manga*] have developed particularly because of the impact of translation strategies adopted by scanlation groups and their impact on current publishers" (221-222). In fact, both the practice of scanlation and its produced artifacts rely on digital and internet tools for their production and dissemination. Furthermore, translation of these manga are also not simply bilingual; according to Rampant, "with a greater availability of Chinese translators many scanlations are produced with Chinese translation acting as the source text" (227). Thus, this translational practice is cooperative, border-crossing, digitally mediated, and motivated by norms that, while not outside the framework of capitalist consumerism, exist uneasily with (and sometimes clash against) it.

One of the main differences in translational practice between 'official' (publisher-sponsored) manga translations and scanlations is their attitude toward domestication of terms, particularly of onomatopoeia. For example, an early Japanese-English translation would provide a domesticated 'tp tp' for the original Japanese *suta-suta*, to indicate footsteps (Rampant 2010, 225). In contrast, Rampant claims that scanlators "do not make allowances for uninitiated readers" (227), instead utilizing multiple strategies, even in the same text; some terms are translated, while others may remain untouched, with "a romanized form of the original Japanese and translated notes…written in gutters or along the border of the page" (227). More recent official translations have responded to these strategies. According to Rampant, more recently, some publishers leave the original sound effects "on the page and put the translation in the margin" (229); others provide a glossary of terms at the beginning of the book, thus foreignizing cultural items (299).

Rampant optimistically professes the power and influence of scanlation: "in the world of manga publishing the successful translation is the one that the audience wants" (231). Yet recent events indicate that the relationship between publishers and fans is still a contested one, with the scanlation community still in flux. As Douglass et al report, publishers radically restricted use of these copyrighted materials in 2010; only time will tell how this translational underground will respond–or if it will survive (201).

Nevertheless, the practice and politics of multi-medial, cross-cultural collaborative translation include complexities that expand the domestic-foreign divide. Groups of scanlators act according to local and shifting norms (with the shared goal of accessing a valued cultural commodity), utilizing sophisticated technologies, and developing cross-national and multilingual networks of individuals based on this goal. Individual scanlators may radically foreignize Japanese terms in their translation as a mode of gate-keeping, demonstrating their own insider knowledge—even as they open access to the material in other ways.

What most strikes me as I look for alternative translational practices, is that scanlators literally leave space in their texts for the untranslatable; the 'Japanese' sound words remain in the *body* of the text, while the translation of these terms is relegated to the margin. The reader of such an expanded text must be willing to be changed in the process of reading, open to encountering 'another language'– just as scanlators are willing to encounter, however virtually, the Others in 'their own' community in order to produce the translations that they desire.

As Wood points out, there are "countless elements that are local and untranslatable; local and translatable; not local at all but not translated; or translated into the most enduring, cosmic terms" (88). Considering all these potential apertures between (and in) translator and text, examining the relational process of translation itself, and the relations between all the various actors involved–people reading, writing, allowing language to work on and through themselves in multiple ways–specificity is crucial. If a translational context allows me space for the untranslatable, how else can I make sense of the "local and untranslatable"? This brings me to the translational challenge of Japanese mimetics.

How (Japanese) Language Needs A Body

As many linguists have observed, mimetics are much more common in a handful of languages, including Japanese, than in most of the world's languages, including English (Inose 2007, 98). Although the exact number is difficult to determine, Baba (2003) asserts that approximately 1600 Japanese mimetics have been catalogued by lexographers (1862). These can be broadly categorized into *giongo* (onomatopoeia), *giseigo* (vocal mimetics), and *gitaigo* (words representing non-auditory senses as well as somatic, emotional, and psychological states). Thus, it is unsurprising given the lack of equivalent terms that both learning Japanese mimetic words and translating them into English can be challenging (Iwasaki et al 2007; Inose 2007). Kita's (1997) theory of the affecto-imagistic dimension of meaning, while not a solution to these problems, certainly sheds light on territory yet to be covered.

According to Kita, language ordinarily functions semantically within the analytic dimension of meaning. However, in contrast, mimetics access an affecto-imagistic dimension, where meaning is instead represented in terms of affect and multi-sensory imagery. In fact, Kita asserts that "[the] affecto-imagistic dimension goes far beyond the expressive function since mimetics signify not only affect but also mental representation of an event of state that is external to a speaker" (402).

In Japanese, mimetics function as phonologically regular words (typically adverbials or nominals), which are usually either monosyllabic or bisyllabic. Furthermore, in utterances *giongo* and *gitaigo* are often accompanied by iconic physical gestures which engage the body, as well as being coupled with prosodic peaks that carry "emotional overtones"–"as if all the affective energy is trapped in the mimetics" (Kita 1997, 397). Thus, Kita concludes:

> An affecto-imagistic representation is an eventuality representation in which perceptual-motor information is temporally organized with contingent affective information…. [This mental information] can also be evoked internally without actual input from the perceptual-motor or affective systems [via a mimetic]…The effect of this evocation is the reexperiencing of the signified eventuality, which leads to the subjective experience of vivid emotional imagery (406).

Returning to Saigan's "*Otsukimi no Yoru*" as an example, I note that there are 54 instances of mimetics (including one non-auditory) in 36 different frames. However, out of the total 15 different onomatopoeia (and one non-auditory mimetic), only 7 had a clear English equivalent; furthermore, those 7 were only used in 11 frames. Excluding vocal mimetics (*giseigo*) such as "ha ha ha" to signify laughing and "hikku" to represent a drunken hiccup, only 3 of the 53 onomatopoeia ("tweet tweet," "tick-tock" and "ding ding ding") were translatable. All the others required multi-word explanations (such as the word *goton goton* indicating the clunking sway of a moving train).

Kita's theory goes a long way in explaining not only why the manga is effective in instilling a sense of nostalgia in me, since "in the affecto-imagistic dimension, various kinds of information from different cognitive modalities remain modality-specific, creating the subjective effect of evoking an image or 're-experience'" (387). It also clarifies why translating the overall affective environment created by the process of reading the manga is so difficult. My sense of nostalgia is heightened, as the experiential directness of the sound imagery contrasts with my knowledge that I have no legitimate access, or connection to, Japanese history. And yet as a participant in specific linguistic and social communities within Japan, with the shared experiential and relational knowledge that accompanied living many years of my life in Tokyo, I feel the connection–I can, linguistically, imagistically, and experientially participate in the world of the manga.

However, when I translate the story, the feelings dissipate, since the language of my translation remains almost totally in the analytic realm, rather than the affecto-imagistic dimension accessed by the rich array of mimetics available in Japanese. While the expressive type and the lovely drawings remain on the page in black and white, I am left to wonder how (or indeed even whether) to share these feelings with another reader of/in English.

Situating Translation as Process

Ultimately, I choose to accept the text's points of resistance to full translation. After all a printed text is much more set, more permanent than one's lived, ephemeral, daily experience. What kind of relationships am I enacting when I read and translate? With whom? What are the material conditions of that relationship-in-process? What are the implications/expected outcomes? What is a translational practice that is capable of performing/reinscribing these specific contexts and relations, rather than idealizing and fixing language into a bodiless mind-space? My body is always there. The bodies of other actual people, who are different from me in various ways, are also there, inviting some sort of engagement.

Approaching the manga story a final time, I find that its use of language-in-visual-narrative both indicates, and enacts, a liminal space where expected (semantic/social) orders are allowed to break down. Examining the instances where the regularity of the mimetic is relaxed, I find the wild, sensually-rich urban space inhabited by the summer insects and *tanuki*–a space that remains outside but regularly within earshot of the domesticated spaces of home, town, and office. This space (descriptively called *susukigahara,* or "pampas grass field," by the *yakitori* shop owner), is not clearly delineated within the cultural narrative of "*Otsukimi no Yoru*" but is instead allowed to float freely, in contrast to the strictly delineated spaces of human connection and obligation. Ironically, it is only a wake-up call from the mythical wild symbolized by the *tanuki* that gives Machida a chance to return from the chaotic space of loss and longing, and re-enter the realm of functional human culture.

In a parallel way, non-totalizing, process-oriented approaches to translation may indicate alternatives to ossified institutional bounds. As Spivak (2005) suggests, a translator must grasp the writer's intentions and "inhabit" the host language (95). I would add that translation also requires a situated, embodied facet, an element of or strategy for locating the translating subject always-in-relation, working to problematize the boundaries between self and other. Spivak's metropolitan translator can make translational practice an object lesson in how languages and people are never fully bounded, independent entities. Rather than aiming for a translated text that is transparent, the process/practice of translation itself should be made transparent.

One risk is that such a translator could end up erring on the side of self-indulgent autobiography. Another risk is that, in inhabiting marginal territories, she may alienate herself too much/too permanently from institutional frameworks. It seems clear that explicitly process-oriented approaches won't work in every genre: e.g., translation of scientific texts where the myth of transparency is expected in creating universal facts. However, challenges to a "unified subject" can, as Spivak suggests (105), counter the 'mastery' narrative of language outlined by Sakai; translation of works in 'artistic' genres can be predicated upon the idea of the encounter, performing the very interpersonal relationships such works aim to create, rather than taking as given totalizing and ungrounded abstraction.

In reading Japanese cultural artifacts, I might then rename nostalgia as *yearning*, a "sensibility that cuts across the boundaries of race, class, gender, and sexual practice" (Braidotti 2011, 22), to promote empathy and solidarity (in a move toward the future) rather than absence and loss (rooted in the past). The differences between people are neither insubstantial nor generalizable, they are encoded and instantiated on multiple levels simultaneously. It seems to me that the while the entry points to communication may be multiple, I must always return to the specific, embodied points of contact between those who have traveled through different spaces, experiencing different viewpoints, yet who have come together to co-create particular moments, to inhabit and share cultural, linguistic spaces and times.

In his 2006 article, Sakai asks, "What might translation be if we suppose that a language is not countable or that one language cannot be easily distinguished from another?" (72). My experience suggests taking this question a step further, to envision what 'translation' might be if we suppose that each *person* is not countable, that one *individual* human cannot be easily separated from another, particularly in communicative contexts that depend on heightened sociality.

As Sakai points out, translation assumes certain kinds of ontological unity–of two languages completely foreign to each other, of speakers who either can or cannot understand both (Sakai 73). In this cofigurative conceptualization, "one unity is figured out, represented and comprehended as a spatial figure, in contrast to another—as if the two unities were already present in actuality" (74). Here the translator is a liminal figure, occupying the position of the text's addressee when reading, yet of the addresser when transmitting the translated text. As such, the translator as always in motion—not simply situated *on* the border but instead *moving in* the spaces where borders are always being reconstructed and reperformed (75). Thus the translator marks an elusive point of discontinuity in the social introducing "an instability into the putatively *personal* relations among the agents of speech, writing, listening and reading. The translator is internally split and multiple, devoid of a stable position. At best they are *subject in transit*" (75).

This instability is ultimately relational, marking "the instability of the *we* as subject rather than the *I*, since the translator cannot be a unified and coherent personality in translation" (75). Instead of valuing "*continuity in discontinuity*," (Sakai 1997, 13, emphasis in original), and thus participating in the schema of co-figuration, which creates and recreates national differences in reiterating the border, a translator-in-transit would consciously and explicitly inhabit that site, embodying and articulating the contradictions inherent in her (multiple) position(s).

This new subjectivity-in-progress is undoubtedly plural, taking different forms under different conditions. A nomadic subject may even herself be different under different conditions, remaining flexible, responsive and creative, loyal to nurturing communities and places but still a polyglot, "capable of some healthy skepticism about steady identities and mother tongues" (Braidotti 2011, 39). Nomadic translation-as-process may also be able to induce such creativity, loyalty and skepticism in others. For, as Braidotti points out, "more conceptual creativity is necessary, more theoretical effort is needed to bring about the conceptual leap across inertia, nostalgia, aporia, and the other forms of critical stasis induced by our historical condition. We need to learn to think differently about the kind of nomadic subjects we have already become and the processes of the deep-seated transformation we are undergoing" (13). Embodied understandings, multiple, situated readings and acceptance of contradiction are all survival skills for practitioners of such future translation. Where, how and by whom these practices will be fully realized remains to be seen.

References

Baba, J. (2003). Pragmatic Function of Japanese Mimetics in the Spoken Discourse of Varying Emotive Intensity Levels. *Journal of Pragmatics,* 35 (12), pp. 1861-1889.

Braidotti, R. (2011). *Nomadic Subjects: Embodiment and Sexual Difference in Contemporary Feminist Theory, Second Edition.* New York: Columbia University Press.

Douglass, J., Huber, W. and Manovich L. (2011). Understanding Scanlation: How to Read One Million Fan-translated Manga Pages. *Image & Narrative,* 12 (1), pp. 190-227.

Inose, H. (2007). Translating Japanese Onomatopoeia and Mimetic Words. In: A. Pym, and A. Perekrestenko, eds., *Translation Research Projects 1.* Tarragona, Spain: Intercultural Studies Group. 97-116.

Ivy, M. (1995). *Discourses of the Vanishing: Modernity, Phantasm, Japan.* Chicago and London: University of Chicago Press.

Iwasaki, N., Vinson, D., and Vigliocco, G. (2007). What Do English Speakers Know About *Gera-gera* and *Yota-yota?*: A Cross-linguistics Investigation of Mimetic Words for Laughing and Walking. *Sekai no Nihongo* Kyōiku 17, pp. 53-78.

Kinsella, S. (2000). *Adult Manga: Culture and Power in Contemporary Japanese Society.* Surrey, UK: Curzon Press.

Kita, S. (1997). Two-dimensional Semantic Analysis of Japanese Mimetics. *Linguistics* 35, (2) pp. 379-415.

Kita, S. (2001). Semantic Schism and Interpretive Integration in Japanese Sentences with a Mimetic: A Reply to Tsujimura. *Linguistics* 39 (2), pp. 419-436.

Potsch, E. and Williams, R. (2012). Image Schemas and Conceptual Metaphor in Action Comics. In: F. Bramlett, ed., *Linguistics and the Study of Comics.* London: Palgrave Macmillan, pp. 13-36.

Rampant, J. (2010). The Manga Polysystem: What Fans Want, Fans Get. In: T. Johnson-Woods. *Manga: An Anthology of Global and Cultural Perspectives.* New York: Continuum Publishing. pp. 221-232.

Saigan R. (2005). *Sanchōme no yūhi: Eigaka tokubetsuhen.* Shogakukan, Tokyo.

Sakai, N. (1997). *Translation & Subjectivity: On "Japan" and Cultural Nationalism.* Minneapolis and London: University of Minnesota Press.

Sakai, N. (2006). Translation. *Theory, Culture & Society* 23 (2-3), pp. 71-86.

Spivak, G. (2005) Translating into English. In: S. Bermann and M. Wood, eds., *Nation, Language, and the Ethics of Translation.* Princeton, NJ: Princeton University Press, pp. 93-110.

Venuti, L. (1995). *The Translator's Invisibility: A History of Translation.* London: Routledge.

Venuti, L. (2005). Local Contingencies: Translation and National Identities. In: S. Bermann and M. Wood, eds., *Nation, Language, and the Ethics of Translation.* Princeton, NJ: Princeton University Press, pp. 177-202.

(2016). *Sanchōme no yūhi.* [online] *Wikipedia.* Available at: https://ja.wikipedia.org/wiki/三丁目の夕日. Accessed 27 December 2016.

(2016). Sunset on Third Street. [online] *Wikipedia.* Available at: https://en.wikipedia.org/wiki/Sunset_on_Third_Street. Accessed 27 December 2016.

Wood, M. (2005). The Languages of Cinema. In: S. Bermann and M. Wood, eds., *Nation, Language, and the Ethics of Translation.* Princeton, NJ: Princeton University Press, pp. 79-88.

Flowers

Ben Highmore
UNIVERSITY OF SUSSEX

I was giddy from the scent. It seemed to drench the small space with heady notes of citrus, interwoven with something pungent, earthy, and rotting. The small shop was crowded with flowers and plants and jewellery and tiny pictures and old furniture. And flowers I had never seen before: roses that seemed to be made from ancient parchments that might turn to dust if you touched them; ivy that seemed to have leaves that would be more likely to rust than to decompose. And colours that you could only find in old books where the images had faded slightly and where the printing was slightly misaligned.

She was telling me her story. Her parents were from Eastern Europe and when she was at school (in England) the teachers encouraged her to go to university. After university she worked in mental health for fifteen years. And now she had this small shop. She didn't want to make much money, had no ambition of this shop being the first of many; she just wanted to work with flowers and to be part of the community. She grew up nearby. Her parents had had a flower shop too. She liked working with flowers and being there at various points in people's lives. Because, well, people need flowers at various times, to celebrate, and to well…

> She looks at me, and says 'I'm sorry I've upset you'.
>
> I try to speak but I can't.
>
> She hugs me and tells me that next time we meet it
> will probably be her that is crying.

I can't say anything. I try. But I can't. I wave and smile as I leave (though I fear it might have looked like a grimace). I'm not unhappy, or sad, but I am crying.

I realised that the last time I had been in a flower shop I had been with my sister and my mother and we were choosing the flowers for my father's funeral. It must have been about three years earlier. That flower shop was very different; much bigger and a lot less idiosyncratic. We were shown into a back room where a man was sitting at a computer (he had a small dog with him that lay at his feet). The man and the dog left and we looked through catalogues at pictures of wreathes and other funereal displays. We were a slightly depleted little family, but we were galvanized and were enjoying each other's company. It wasn't a miserable time, even if it was full of grief. And the smell of flowers was, no doubt, similarly overwhelming. There is always that peaty, boggy smell that provides the descant to that fluttery trill of sweetness; always the slight sickly smell that accompanies cascades of effervescent perfumes. But in that large shop, perhaps simply because it was so much bigger, there wasn't that same sense that putrefaction had settled into the midst of such spectacular beauty.

The sense of smell and taste are the most vivid of mnemonic vehicles. Today I can smell particularly pungent industrial cleaners and I am a fourteen year old, muddy and wet in a changing room trying to get warm. I know the density of the tiled flooring, I know the cloying sense of these damp clothes, I know the wooden slats of the seating. Smell and taste transport you quickly, emphatically, completely, even if afterwards you are left searching for the content of that transportation. Was I simply transported to a moment three years earlier, a moment of mourning? Perhaps, yes. But is that all? Wasn't there also that heady smell, so condensed, so complex, that wills us to mourn our own mortality even in the midst of vigorous life? And wasn't there also, and not as a minor aside, someone telling me about how to live a life that wants to connect to the perpetual flows of birth and death, of marriage, of success, of disappointment, of new seasons, of celebration and condolence that rhymes us all. Someone telling me that they want to supply fleeting fragrances and ephemeral bouquets to accompany our passage through life, and is prepared to create a small room where a strange man can walk in off the street to buy a bunch of flowers to celebrate a friend's success and walk out in tears.

A Tiny Library

Ben Highmore
UNIVERSITY OF SUSSEX

At school there was no real encouragement to read. Outside of the set-texts (*Tess of the d'Urbervilles*, *Hard Times*, *The Sword of Honour*, and so on), and endless text books for geography, biology, and on and on, our main reading consisted of comics and pulp novels (the kind that were made into 'spaghetti westerns'). There was no television. It was a boarding school and we were encouraged (or more precisely forced) to take part in sporting activities that took place every afternoon and lasted hours. These were organized not according to age but according to the 'house' you lived in: in this way burly eighteen year olds played football and hockey with (and against) pre-pubescent thirteen year olds. It was organised violence of course.

Life in this school (and, I imagine, in most boarding schools) was organised in a way that meant that privacy was non-existent. Everyone ate together. You washed in a large room that contained four baths and ten basins. The dormitory must have had thirty beds in it. The result was not a feeling of collectivism but resulted in endlessly nuanced corpuscular groupings of twos and threes, sometimes more, and often less. When Tom Harrisson started Mass-Observation in 1937 and decided he would practice anthropology amongst the 'tribes' of Northern England he was not (as critics often think) importing a form of attention that he had learnt on the islands of Melanesia. He was extending his understanding of a tribalism that he had experienced in an English boarding school.

Because it was so rare, privacy was used in these schools as some form of reward. It was a relative condition though. In fact it wasn't privacy you were offered, it was something like 'less-than-total-public-ness' that was on offer. As you went through the school your spatial relations changed. When you started out the only space that 'belonged' to you was a small locker and a bed. You sat on benches around massive tables. A 'reward' for lasting a year, or for being 'good', resulted in you having your own desk in the huge and crowded 'lower room'. The next step-up was a desk in a smaller (and less populated) 'middle room'. The ultimate 'prize' was a study that you shared with one or two others (but if you were very unlucky this might mean sharing a small space with some psychotic boy you hated and who, more importantly, hated you). Aloneness was not something that was generally available and was not something that was prized. What was prized was the sort of space that a corpuscle of boys could inhabit that would keep them safe from a phalanx of malign marauders.

To find aloneness meant seeking out spaces that were outside the usual designated space, outside the general battlegrounds of our communal life. For me smoking provided a geography of solitude. Finding places to smoke meant searching out neglected spaces, or spaces that remained unvisited at certain parts of the day. It meant wandering beyond the confines of the school. But the best place for aloneness (but not for smoking) turned out to be right in the centre of the house, on the borderland between the 'house master's' private home (a place where you might be invited, but couldn't voluntarily enter) and the public space of the house where all the boys lived. This borderland room was a very small library consisting of a few chairs, a table, perhaps an old sofa, a radiator (a source of heat was always a good idea) and books.

It is hard for me to imagine my relationship to books without thinking about spaces like this: small spaces, often dark in colour (this room was dark green), with clanky radiators. I remember the books I found there: books by Samuel Beckett, by Virginia Woolf, and by Jean-Paul Sartre (like other fourteen year olds I found the *Roads to Freedom* trilogy to be a compelling and sleazy soap opera); books by Dostoyevsky. The shelves were scattered with 'Penguin Classics' and 'Penguin Modern Classics' and books published by John Calder (in amongst a more austere collection detailing military campaigns and the lives of monarchs). It was a quiet, warm, secluded space. A place rarely visited. A space where you remained unfound. I can't help but think of the spatiality of books in this way. Wherever the stories seem to roam, however expansive the timescale of a plot is, books provide their own small, dark green and warm rooms. Places to be unfound in.

The geography of school is seared into my psyche. I wander these spaces in my dreams. The corridors of the study block, the stairwells where you signed-up for games, the middle and lower rooms, the bathrooms and dormitories, supply the scenography for my oneiric life. I have never once dreamed of this tiny library.

Destroy 2000 Yeas of Culture
Unknown, i.imgur.com/47AHR1g.gif

Do You Want Vaporwave,
or Do You Want the Truth?

Cognitive Mapping of Late Capitalist Affect
in the Virtual Lifeworld of Vaporwave

~~~~~~~

Alican Koc
UNIVERSITY OF TORONTO

In "Postmodernism, or, The Cultural Logic of Late Capitalism," Frederic Jameson (1991) mentions an "aesthetic of cognitive mapping" as a new form of radical aesthetic practice to deal with the set of historical situations and problems symptomatic of late capitalism. For Jameson (1991), cognitive mapping functions as a tool for postmodern subjects to represent the totality of the global late capitalist system, allowing them to situate themselves within the system, and to reenact the critique of capitalism that has been neutralized by postmodernist confusion. Drawing upon a close reading of the music and visual art of the nostalgic internet-based "vaporwave" aesthetic alongside Jameson's postmodern theory and the affect theory of Raymond Williams (1977) and Brian Massumi (1995; 1998), this essay argues that vaporwave can be understood as an attempt to aestheticize and thereby map out the affective climate circulating in late capitalist consumer culture. More specifically, this paper argues that through its somewhat obsessive hypersaturation with retro commodities and aesthetics from the 1980s and 1990s, vaporwave simultaneously critiques the salient characteristics of late capitalism such as pastiche, depthlessness, and waning of affect, and enacts a nostalgic longing for a modernism that is fleeing further and further into an inaccessible history.

KEYWORDS

Affect, Postmodernism, Late Capitalism, Cognitive Mapping, Aesthetics

Purgatory

A widely shared image on the Internet asks viewers to reflect on the atrocities of the past century. Providing no information on its creator or whereabouts, the grainy image depicts a stark grey concrete wall with "HiROSHiMA '45 CHERNOBYL '86 WiNDOWS '95" hastily grafittied onto it in black spray paint, evoking a sense of urgency to the message. The message is intended as a kind of black humour in the Apple-saturated and dehistoricized postmodern consumer world of the present. We get the joke – that the Internet medium through which we are viewing this image has contributed to a suppression of history through which Hiroshima, Chernobyl, and Windows 95 may as well have been comparable in their historical significance and respective contributions to human suffering (Jameson, 1991).

Yet at the same time, the image seems saturated with haunting affects that come to life as you meditate on it. The former two events cited in the image evoke affects of inconceivable suffering and catastrophe, brought into the collective consciousness through black-and-white images of mutation, rubble, and ruin, but somewhat obscured through history, and a bleakly warming sense of cultural otherness. "Good thing I wasn't there," the viewer might think. On the other hand, the latter event brings to life a different sort of affect that is likely more familiar to the image's viewers: a kind of throbbing of the "ordinary, chronic, and cruddy" forms of suffering that characterizes late capitalist life as it freezes and glitches, prompting one to try to "ctrl-alt-del" or "restart", knowing full well that things would never be the same after that God-forsaken operating system, at least not for a while (Povinelli, 2011, p. 54).

Toward the end of Fredric Jameson's 1984 essay, "Postmodernism, or The Cultural Logic of Late Capitalism", which also functions as the first chapter to his eponymous book, Jameson (1991, p. 46) argues that attempts to make moralizing judgments on postmodernism are a "category mistake". According to Jameson (1991), cultural critics and moralists of postmodernity are too deeply involved in its cultural categories to enact a traditional ideological critique. Jameson (1991, p. 48-49) aptly notes the demoralizing and depressing "moment of truth" of postmodernism in which the radical edge of previous Leftist conceptions of cultural politics has dulled or rusted due to the fact that these politics can no longer achieve a "critical distance" from the system they wish to critique. For Jameson, the solution to this seems to be found in a new form of radical aesthetic practice dealing with the fresh set of historical situations and problems symptomatic of late capitalism. Drawing on Kevin Lynch's idea of disalienating urban space through one's own mental mapping of the city, and Louis Althusser's notion of ideology as, "the representation of the subject's *Imaginary* relationship to his or her *Real* conditions of existence", Jameson (1991, p. 51) calls for a radical practice he refers to as an "aesthetic of cognitive mapping". For Jameson (1991), cognitive mapping can be understood as a tool for postmodern subjects to represent the totality of the global late capitalist system, allowing them to situate their subject position within it, and to reenact the critique of capitalism that had previously been neutralized by postmodernist confusion.

Jameson's idea of representing the totality of the myriad of processes in late capitalism has drawn fire from a numbers of critics, as noted in Robert T. Tally Jr.'s (2000) "Jameson's Project of Cognitive Mapping: A Critical Engagement", which notes the poststructuralist line of questioning around who is doing the representing and what is being represented. Tally Jr.'s (2000, p. 414) work also takes very literally the Lynchian influence in Jameson's work, seeing cognitive mapping as the first step in what he terms "cartographics", a "set of critical practices that would engage with issues of space and spatial relations in connection with cultural and social theory". Rather than understanding the cartography of cognitive mapping in a necessarily physical geographical sense, I want to argue here, drawing on Jameson's (2000) assertion that cognitive mapping is "nothing but a code word for 'class consciousness'", that cognitive mapping can also be understood as the mapping of an affective space produced by late capitalist culture. Specifically, this essay will be looking at the phenomenon of vaporwave, an Internet aesthetic from the early 2010s founded on a nostalgic fascination with mainstream cultural aesthetics of the 1980s and 1990s, as a possible attempt at creating an aesthetic of cognitive mapping. As I will argue, vaporwave reproduces a melancholy affect through its aestheticization of the depthlessness, waning of affect, new technologies, pastiche, and collapse of high/low categories into consumer culture that define postmodernism for Jameson. Vaporwave aesthetics can thus be understood as creating a cognitive map of the bleak affective space of late capitalism, inviting viewers or listeners to step inside and critique it from within.

Remember I Was Vapor, Remember I Was Just Like You

How's this for a cognitive map: a hot pink background with a black and pink tiled dance floor stretching into the infinite, evoking the Black Lodge from the last episode of David Lynch's (1991) *Twin Peaks* television series, or perhaps the dance floor on which George Michael (1984) had his last faithful dance with his star-crossed lover immortalized in "Careless Whisper". At the forefront of the image on its left side sits a bust of Helios, the personification of the sun in Greek mythology, staring back at the viewer as if to serve as a satirical reminder of what "aesthetics" once referred to.

Album artwork, *Floral Shoppe* (フローラルの専門店), Macintosh Plus, 2011

The "beauty question" is also referenced to the right of Helios in a window to a better world: a cheesily melancholy image of a boat sailing through the sky's golden reflection over the water toward a city skyline. Above it reads "MACフローラルの専門店" in a fluorescent green font. As you stare at the image, music begins to play – a slowed-down rendition of Diana Ross' 1984 single, "It's Your Move" that sounds like a retrospective on 80s pop music by way of Houston, Texas' codeine-fueled "chopped and screwed" music style seeps out, vapor-like, permeating the air with a musical equivalent to cheap perfume. The song's title is "リサフランク420 / 現代のコンピュー (Risafuranku 420/Gendai no Konpyū Lisa Frank 420/Modern Computing)" by Macintosh Plus, an alias of electronic artist Vektroid.

So what is this and what does it all mean? Vaporwave refers to an audio-visual Internet aesthetic characterized by a fascination with retro cultural aesthetics. Following on the heels of the short-lived micro-cultures of "seapunk" and "chillwave" on Tumblr in the early 2010s, vaporwave draws from a bizarre canon of nostalgic imagery of the 1980s and 1990s (Beks, n.d.). Taking its name from a spoof on "vaporware", a practice of promoting nonexistent products adopted by computer companies to keep competitors at bay, vaporwave employs a corny depiction of retro imagery to evoke capitalist sleaze, working to expose the emptiness underlying the glossy sheen of late consumer capitalism (Lhooq, 2013). In attempting to create a sensationalized depiction of late capitalist alienation, vaporwave art uses neon colours, Windows 95 glitch art, corporate logos, images of Greek and Roman busts, melancholy 8-bit images of cityscapes, beaches, and other quasi-utopian aesthetic "elsewheres", and Japanese anime and text. As a musical genre, vaporwave has been variously referred to as "chillwave for Marxists," "post-elevator music," and "corporate smooth jazz Windows 95 pop", using heavily manipulated samples of forgotten corporate music from the 1980s such as pop ballads, elevator music, smooth jazz, and computer and video game scores to create alienating reinterpretations of familiar sounds (Lhooq, 2013; Beks, n.d.). Conceptually, vaporwave music attempts to evoke the generic atmosphere of the mundane temples of global late capital, such as the office lobby, the hotel reception area, the mall, the beach resort, and the corporatized plaza (Harper, 2012).

While vaporwave has traditionally been understood as a critique of late capitalist consumer culture, its exact theoretical influences have been disputed. In an influential essay titled "Vaporwave and the Pop-Art of the Virtual Plaza", Adam Harper (2012) notes that vaporwave's capitalist critique can be understood in the context of accelerationism, the philosophy of pushing capitalism toward its inevitably violent conclusion developed by British philosopher Nick Land in the 1990s. As Harper (2012) writes, vaporwave musicians, "let flow the music that lubricates Capital, open the door to a monstrously alienating sublime, twist dystopia into utopia and vice versa, and dare you not to like it". Harper (2012) cites an interview conducted with vaporwave artist James Ferraro, in which Ferraro argues that realism and idealism "bounce off one another repeatedly in a paradigm" in the late capitalist moment, and that he applauds the future rather than fearing it. However, in an interview with the prolific vaporwave artist, Robin Burnett, better known as INTERNET CLUB, Burnett expresses a desire to do something "Debordian" by creating a "the defamiliarisation of things we've become so use to that we don't notice them any more" (Harper, 2012).

Contrary to Harper's analysis, Burnett's reference to Guy Debord, the leader of the neo-Marxist Situationist International signifies an undeniably idealistic desire to disrupt the everyday spectacles of capitalist society, rather than to accelerate them. Yet, Harper (2012) also cites psychoanalytic and Marxist influences in vaporwave's name, drawing on the concept of sublimation in Freudian thinking, and Marx's quote from the *Communist Manifesto*, in which he states that "all that is solid melts into air" – referring to the constant changes to society under capitalism. Surprisingly missing amid the theoretically confused party of accelerationists, situationists, psychoanalysts and Marxists credited with influencing vaporwave's late capitalist critique is Fredric Jameson. As I will argue, the characteristic traits of postmodernism that Jameson identifies in his eponymously titled book are not only evident in vaporwave aesthetics, but function in creating a cognitive map of the affective space of late capitalism. I will now turn briefly to a summary of the affect theory that informs this argument, before reading some of Jameson's arguments in *Postmodernism* in relation to vaporwave aesthetics and the affects they produce.

Hit Vibes

In his essay, "The Autonomy of Affect", Brian Massumi (1995, p. 96) draws on Deleuze and Guattari's adoption of the term "affect" from Spinoza, defining affects as "virtual synaesthetic perspectives anchored in…the actually existing, particular things that embody them". For Massumi (1995, p. 91), affects thus refer to a set of deeply embodied presubjective vibrations that exist simultaneously in actual life, as well as what Massumi terms the "virtual": a paradoxical realm of potentiality in which intensities that cannot otherwise be experienced can be felt. Massumi (1995) distinguishes affect from emotion, using the latter to refer to socially or personally qualified feelings rooted in the actual, and describing the former as a set of prepersonal feelings that defies perception and articulation through its transcendence of the actual. While the autonomy of affect for Massumi exists in its ability to escape perception, articulation, and subsequently, more traditional materially-oriented means of social analysis, affect carries important ramifications in thinking about both politics and aesthetics. Massumi (1995) cites the powerful feelings of confusion and awe surrounding Ronald Reagan's mimetic communication style, and Reagan's subsequent two-term presidency as one of the first instances of the mobilization of affect in postmodern politics. For Massumi (1995), the rapid rate at which information is circulated in the postmodern period signifies the end of ideology in defining the global functioning of power, and heralds the growing need for scholars and politicians of the left to begin thinking about politics affectively.

At first glance, Massumi's, (2009, p. 7) assertion that ideology no longer functions as the global mode of power, and his echoing of Deleuze and Guattari in stating that, "no situation is ever fully predetermined by ideological structures or codings" seems at odds with Fredric Jameson's explicitly Marxist project of cognitive mapping. Indeed, for Jameson (2000, p. 418), who refers to his aesthetic of cognitive mapping as "nothing but a code word for 'class consciousness'", this project functions as an effort to revive a Marxist capacity to struggle by giving individual subjects a sense of their place within late capitalism's global system. In stark contrast to Jameson's desire to map the connections between the late capitalist system and its aesthetics, Massumi's intellectual forebear, Gilles Deleuze opposes the tendency to draw straightforward correlations between facets of culture and their respective origins, economic or otherwise. As Deleuze (1994 p. 176 & 193) states in *What Is Philosophy?*, "art is the language of sensations", yet "no art and no sensation have ever been representational" of reality. Put beside the sassy anti-representational aesthetics of the hip new poststructuralists on the block, Fredric Jameson begins to look like kind of a square: an old Marxist clinging desperately to seemingly outdated models of base and superstructure amid the influx of hot new discourses complicating these relationships.

Like Deleuze and Massumi, Raymond Williams presents a compelling mode of examining the relationship between affect and aesthetics. In Williams' (1977, p. 133) case, this is what he terms "structures of feeling", referring to a particular set of feelings specific to a time and place that informs formal and stylistic conventions in art. Like Massumi's affects, these structures indicate a mode of feeling and thinking that exists "in an embryonic phase before it can become fully articulate", that are otherwise unintelligible through the study of fixed social forms and exist in a complex relationship to the already articulate (Williams, 1977, p. 130-131). Like Jameson however, Williams' (1977, p. 133) aesthetics also function as a part of a Marxist project, seeking to enhance the traditional base and superstructure model by describing the rich sets of feelings produced in this dynamic in a capitalist system, and treating "forms and conventions in art and literature as inalienable elements of a social material process". In situating the mapping of art's affects within the Marxist base and superstructure model, Williams' structure of feelings concept thus functions in reconciling some of the tension between a Marxist aesthetic of cognitive mapping and poststructuralist theories of affect.

In "Post-Cinematic Affect: On Grace Jones, Boarding Gate and Southland Tales", Steven Shaviro (2010) also draws a parallel between Jameson and Deleuze by noting the scholars' insistence on mapping their respectively unrepresentable terrains of late capitalism and affect. For Shaviro (2010, p. 6-7), both scholars seek to "know" their respective systems in a non-representational way that he terms "an aesthetic of affective mapping". Drawing on Williams' correlation between affect and aesthetics in his "structure of feelings" concept, Shaviro (2010, p. 2) refers to "a kind of ambient, free-floating sensibility that permeates our society today" that accounts for "what it feels like to live in the early twenty-first century". For the purposes of this essay, I will refer to the aestheticization of late capitalism's affects mapped in vaporwave as a "virtual lifeworld", borrowing Massumi's term. Like Shaviro's (2010, p. 7) "aesthetic of affective mapping", the notion of a virtual lifeworld refers to a loose aestheticization of feelings circulating within a particular space and/or time, mapped across a diverse array of expressions. In the case of vaporwave, I will argue that the virtual lifeworld being mapped is one characterized by a uniquely postmodern affect of melancholic nostalgia. As I will try to show, this effect is largely created through an aestheticization of the feelings of estrangement produced by the salient characteristics of late capitalism outlined by Jameson, and the hinting at a sense of nostalgia for a romanticized time in the early late capitalist period.

A New Day

The first characteristic of postmodernism that Jameson (1991) outlines is the emergence of depthlessness or superficiality as a formal feature in art. Here, Jameson (1991) uses Andy Warhol's pop art as an example of an uncritical, and even fetishistic approach to commodification, which challenges a modernist approach to art interpretation by creating a work with no lead into a hermeneutic analysis. The "you-get-what-you-see" tendency of postmodern art that Jameson notes is also one that is actively called attention to and satirized in vaporwave aesthetics. Here, Warhol's uncritical presentation of the commodity in its raw form is taken to its limits with a somewhat obsessive hypersaturation of nostalgic commodities in vaporwave visual art. In one notable example, this takes the shape of a purple image of a sunset over the water, pasted with pictures of Fiji water bottles, cans of Arizona ice tea, the Nintendo 64 logo, Japanese anime characters, and in the centre of it, a series of Windows 95 windows all displaying tacky Internet stickers on a hot pink screen, their tabs all titled with the question, "IS THIS ART?"

The forceful reiteration of the latter question seems to indicate a desperate critique of postmodern art's superficiality, while the constant citation of nostalgic commodities like the outdated Nintendo 64 console both mock this superficiality and signify a kind of longing for a retro elsewhere. While Warhol's depthless art seems to defy hermeneutic analysis through its unadorned presentation of ordinary commodities, vaporwave art is saturated with Japanese text in order to depict a globalized future that is alien and impenetrable to its presupposed demographic of white Western viewers (Lhooq, 2013). Vaporwave music also places an emphasis on the banal, mundane, and everyday that would likely surpass Warhol's sensibilities. Eco Virtual's *Atmospheres第1*, which is themed around weather forecast music serves as a good example of the latter. With its soft, clicky beats, smooth jazz saxophones, sparse piano notes, and song titles like "Acid Rain", and "Tropical Depression", Eco Virtual turns the numbing mundanity of weather forecasts into a powerful critique of a world in which mental illness and environmental hazards are transformed into commodified everyday occurrences that are accompanied by soulless music and images of blue skies.

The depthlessness of postmodernism is closely linked to what Jameson (1991, p. 15) terms the "waning of affect", following the death of the modern subject. As Jameson (1991) argues, the organizational bureaucracy of the postmodern world has lead to the dissolution of the centred modernist subject that existed in the period of classical capitalism and the nuclear family. Here, Jameson (1991) famously cites Edvard Munch's *The Scream* as a modernist expression of alienation and anxiety no longer appropriate it the world of postmodernity. It must be noted here that the notion of a waning of affect characterizing the postmodern condition may at first seem contradictory to my emphasis on the affective space of postmodernism that is being depicted by vaporwave aesthetics. This is noted by Brian Massumi (1995), who argues against Jameson's assertion by claiming that if anything, late capitalist culture is characterized by a surfeit of affect. The distinction between Jameson and Massumi's conceptions of affect must be noted here. While for Jameson, affect is related to the subject, falling under what Massumi would term emotion, Massumi's notion of affect is presubjective, and primary to emotion. In this regard, the waning of affect that Jameson refers to serves as a contributing factor to what I refer to as an affect of mundanity in vaporwave's depiction of the virtual lifeworld of late capitalism, drawing on a more Massumian conception of the term. This is to say that the banal affects produced by vaporwave's shallow and soulless aesthetic can be understood as a reaction to the turn away from a modernist aesthetic of expression as exemplified *The Scream*. In the virtual lifeworld of vaporwave, the wild cries of the exasperated modernist subject have been replaced by dull, inarticulate expressions of a mundane collective suffering. Instead of the manic state of existential horror brought to life by "the cry, the raw vibrations of the human throat", the vaporwave lifeworld presents its "broken dreams and silent screams" in

technicoloured hues, evoking a faded memory of a time predating the unemotional starkness of postmodernity – a place in a long lost past captured on a discarded VHS cassette, a place where colourful expressions and frenzied cries of hope and purpose would burst across the cultural landscape (Jameson, 1991, p. 13).

For Jameson (1991, p. 37), the technological advances of late capitalism can be understood as a contributing factor to the "crisis of temporality" that characterizes postmodernity. The prominence of the Internet in late capitalism has played a significant role in accelerating the "blank parody" of pastiche, pushing history further and further away as we attempt to seek it through our own representations and simulations of it (Jameson, 1991, p. 17). "DESTROY 2000 YEARS OF CULTURE", reads one particularly poignant image of a trio of depressed-looking statues in seeming response to Jameson.

In addition to pastiche, the image also evokes an aesthetic question as it appears in the neon-coloured, dehistoricized postmodern world of vaporwave. Vaporwave's visual aesthetic has been a long-running joke throughout its short-lived history.

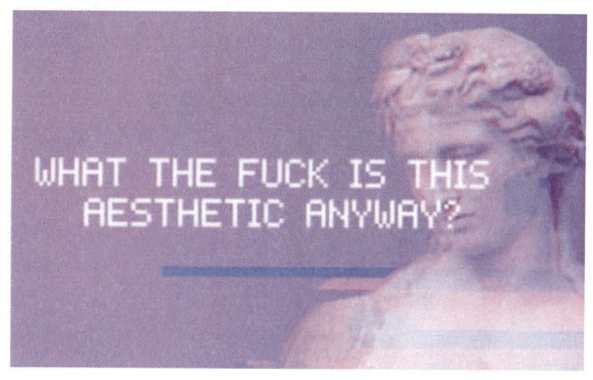

While never explicitly citing its theoretical sources, the prominence of Greco-Roman statues and columns in vaporwave seems to function as a tongue-in-cheek reference to the critiques of discourses of beauty and fine art in Kantian aesthetics undertaken by Marxist cultural theorists. In *Marxism and Literature*, Williams (1977) mentions that the replacement of the disciplines of grammar and rhetoric with that of criticism created a mode of aesthetic criticism whose emphasis on the aesthetic function as sublimity and beauty in works of literature served to distinguish the bourgeoisie from lower class consumers of non-literature. Following the critiques of theorists such as Williams and Terry Eagleton, numerous scholars such as Michael Bérubé (2005, p. 16) have embraced a "populist strain of cultural studies", searching for beauty and intellectual material in popular cultural texts, and effectively dissolving the modernist distinction between high culture and mass culture into a uniform commercial culture (Jameson, 1991). In vaporwave aesthetics, the employment of Greco-Roman sculptures and columns then seem to function as tombstones of sorts, recalling a dim memory of stability in the respective definitions of aesthetics, beauty, and fine art predating the cultural tornado of postmodernism. Similarly, the prominence of dated cultural artifacts associated with early postmodernity like the original PlayStation console or the Nintendo Game Boy can be understood as portals into a more innocent time of postmodernity for the millennial viewer, before technology and late capitalist culture fully reduced history into a uniform blur accessible only through pastiche.

The aforementioned period of postmodernity which roughly spans the late 1980s through the mid-1990s plays an important role in the nostalgic melancholia of vaporwave's virtual lifeworld. Following Jameson, this paper uses the terms "postmodernity" and "late capitalism" interchangeably, referring loosely to their circulation and discussion in the postwar period. By referring to the late 1980s and early 1990s as a period of "early postmodernity" cited in vaporwave's aesthetic, it should be noted that I am referring to the period immediately predating the dramatic changes in late capitalist life facilitated through digital technologies such as the widespread access to home computers and the Internet. It is interesting to note here that the historical period represented in vaporwave not only corresponds to the childhoods of vaporwave's presupposed Western millennial subjects, but also the time at which Jameson was most actively theorizing postmodernity. In the virtual lifeworld of vaporwave, the presupposed millennial subject constantly seeks to flee the feelings of isolation and numbness generated by postmodernity's detachment from history, depthlessness, and muted expression, by returning to a warm place in their childhood preceding the trauma that followed postmodernity's final fracture from history through digital technology, and subsequent departure into its pastiche-fueled, "schizophrenic" eternal present (Jameson, 1991, p. xi). By ransacking the treasury of technological artifacts, cultural relics, and quotidian objects of this period, vaporwave's aesthetic appears to be attempting to reestablish contact with history by salvaging the long lost fragments of modernity's captivatingly expressive affects. Upon encountering these nostalgic objects however, things become distorted – the objects lose their  historical context, familiar songs or episodes from television programs bleed into one another, and the subject comes to realize the futility in trying to access the past in the schizophrenic eternal present of postmodernity. A 2016 YouTube phenomenon called "Simpsonwave", serves as an excellent example of this, incorporating vaporwave soundtracks over mashed up and distorted footage from The Simpsons. "I'm just a kid…", echoes Blank Banshee's "Teen Pregnancy" track over clips of a stoned-looking Bart embarking on a psychedelic walk through Springfield in a video entitled, "S U N D A Y S C H O O L" by Simpsonswave originator, Lucien Hughes (2016). Here, the viewer is encouraged to step into Bart's shoes, attempting to escape a series of melancholic memories by navigating through a space that is at once familiar yet foreign.

The video's powerful affective grasp on the viewer seems here to be the contradiction between the viewing subject's attempts to once again return to the place of childish innocence embodied by Bart as he navigates the familiar terrain of his hometown, and their subsequent inability to do so in the warped postmodern rendering of the show. Throughout the video, episodes from several early episodes of the show are melded together and distorted with fake television static evoking fading memories, while a mashup between Grandmaster Flash and the Furious Five and Boards of Canada plays overtop. The message seems clear: in mapping the nostalgic affects of postmodernity's schizophrenic haze, vaporwave seems to function like The Eagles' proverbial Hotel California, reminding its guests that they can check out anytime they like, but they can never leave (1976).

DREAMISLAND

We begin our voyage of mapping the virtual lifeworld of late capitalism like De Certeau (1984) did in New York, gazing at the space from above. In this instance, it's a monolithic cityscape, illuminated by a rich 8-bit purple glow with stars gleaming in the sky. It's almost perfect. Drifting over the city, in all lower case letters hovers a deliciously apt question, "where are you?" Good question. Everywhere we walk, the city's streets are deserted.

There are traces of activity here and there – the lights are on in a couple of apartments, a pop can sits littered on the sidewalk, a message spray painted on a wall by an anonymous vandal tells you to "Fuck off" – yet there's nobody on the streets. Perhaps they're at home on their computers. Maybe they're at the mall.

Is this what Jameson (1991, p. 37) meant when he described the "technological sublime" of the new decentred postmodern space? Yet what about this space is sublime? A deep sense of melancholy permeates the air – the few characters that wander around are fallen heroes whimpering depressed monologues on "the tragedy of existence" into their sleeves.

Upon exiting the space, the entire cityscape begins to fall apart – "DON'T WORRY, YOUR DREAMS WILL EVENTUALLY DIE – IT'S ONLY 2 AM ANYWAY". Perhaps it was all a dream. Or maybe just a glitch. What's the difference, really?

I am arguing in this essay that the cognitive map of vaporwave aesthetics seems to be one that focuses on the bleak, melancholy affects of late capitalism. This lifeworld evokes both the feelings of alienation and emptiness of late capitalism, as well as a deep sense of longing for a modernist sense of historicity, meaning, and expression. While a historical comprehension of modernity is lost in the postmodern moment, the obsessive citation of early postmodern technology such as VHS, cassette tapes, outdated video game consoles like the Sony PlayStation, Nintendo Game Boy, and of course, the Windows 95 operating system, seems to function as an index to the final moment of departure into the hyperreality of the late capitalist moment for millennial creators of vaporwave art. Similarly, these objects seem to harken the listener back to a time immediately preceding the completion of the entrance into the postmodern moment in which the promises of technological sublimity and global connectivity in a late capitalist utopia were still vaguely believable. If postmodernism proves itself incapable of "imagining those great utopias that have occasionally broken on the status quo like a sunburst", as Jameson (2003, p. 704) puts it, it can at least provide a melancholic

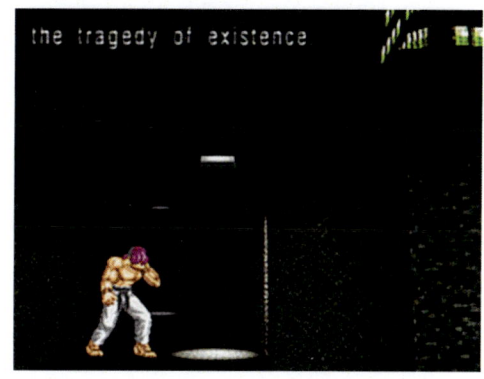

meditation on the "memories on the horizon" of a temporal elsewhere in which utopianism was believable. In doing so, I argue that vaporwave exposes the emptiness of late capitalism, presenting an alienating hypersaturation of its own defining characteristics and using them as a form of critique by situating its audiences in a totalizing atmosphere of nostalgic melancholia. Jameson (1992, p. 18) himself alludes to this sense of nostalgia in his discussion of postmodern "nostalgia films", noting how the latter seeks to create romantic visions of a bygone history to refract the "desperate attempt to appropriate a missing past". Like the neon lit streets of small town America in *American Graffiti*, which Jameson (1992) chooses as an early example of this phenomenon, each space in the virtual lifeworld of vaporwave, be it the aforementioned city skylines and empty streets depicted in its images, or the malls and hotels turned into soundscapes functions as a piece of the cognitive map, working to map out the totality of a uniquely postmodern affect.

This brings us to the final question that I would like to deal with in this paper – the question of totality. More specifically, in keeping with Jameson's (1991) assertion that the aesthetic of cognitive mapping should function in exposing the totality of late capitalism, can it be argued that vaporwave achieves this effect? This is ultimately to ask whether the affect of late capitalist melancholia is capable of accounting for the totality of processes, affective and otherwise under late capitalism. The answer here seems to be both yes and no. In the case of the latter answer, the aforementioned poststructuralist questioning outlined by Robert T. Tally Jr. points to the difficulty of representing totality and the important assertion that that what is represented as the totality of late capitalism will alter as it is represented by different groups and scholars (2000). For example, John Beverly's essay, "Pedagogy and Subalternity: Mapping the Limits of Academic Knowledge" draws on Gayatri Spivak's assertion that the subaltern cannot speak to argue that Jameson's notion of cognitive mapping responds to new epistemologies of capital by attempting to know and thereby othering the subaltern subject (2000). Similarly, in "Mapping the Spaces of Capital", Crystal Bartolovich calls attention to Jameson's description of the imperial stage of capitalism to accuse his theory of totality of excluding and ignoring imperial subjects in India and Jamaica for whom this notion might not be so liberatory (2000).

While all of the critiques of the cognitive mapping project aptly take up some of the issues in representing totality, they seem to take too literally Jameson's notion of the term. In the introduction to *The Geopolitical Aesthetic: Cinema and Space in the World System*, Jameson responds to the question of totality by noting the reemergence of allegory in the postmodern era (1992). Allegory for Jameson (1992, p. 4), functions as the solution to this problem, by allowing "the most random, minute, or isolated landscapes to function as a figurative machinery in which questions about the system and its control over the local ceaselessly rise and fall". As Jameson (1992, p. 114) writes later in the book, "The social totality can be sensed, as it were, from the outside, like a skin at which the Other looks". While the melancholy affects brought to life in the virtual lifeworld of vaporwave speak to the decidedly privileged class positions of late capitalist consumers and artists rather than subaltern subjects, they bring to life an allegory of late capitalist suffering from a place under the skin. This is not "class consciousness" in a traditional Marxian sense, but rather an opening into the virtual realm of late capitalism, the identification of a throbbing affect lodged deep in the collective sentiment of a social body, and one that might provide some clues on how to enact a greater Marxist critique of late capitalism next time around. As Brian Massumi (1995, p. 105-106) writes, "In North America at least, the far right is far more attuned to the imagistic potential of the postmodern body than the established left, and has exploited that advantage for the last decade and a half. Philosophies of affect, potential, and actualization may aid in finding counter-tactics".

HIGHWAYDREAMS(朝の高速道路)1984

I close this essay with a final image, entitled *Driving till the end...* by Argentinian artist Kidmograph. A racecar is driving along the highway through the desert. The road is completely empty, allowing the car to drive right between the two lanes. Playing in the car is a vaporwave soundtrack, perhaps ASHITAKA(アシタカ)'s *HIGHWAYDREAMS*(朝の高速道路)*1984* album.

The opening track is a slowed down and vaguely druggy-sounding take on some piano-driven Japanese adult contemporary music. It's kind of corny, but appropriate for the melancholy feel of the moment. The driver doesn't have a specific destination in mind, and there's nobody around, but some palm trees and greenery have begun to emerge on the sides of the road after miles of desert. More importantly, the road seems to lead straight into the middle of a spectacular sunset, painting the horizon in warm shades of pink, orange, and magenta. This "elsewhere" looks a lot like a faded memory, yet paradoxically offers what looks like the promise of a brighter future on the horizon. And that's exactly where the driver is going.

References

ASHITAKA(アシタカ), 2015. *H I G H W A Y D R E A M S(朝の高速道路)1 9 8 4* [Cassette]. Florida: DMT Tapes.

Bartolovich, C. (2000). Mapping the spaces of capital. In: R.G. Paulston, ed., *Social cartography: mapping ways of seeing social and educational change*. New York & London: Garland Publishing Inc., pp. 375-398.

Basilio, B. (2015). *Vaporwave – where are you*. September 14. Available at: https://www.themebeta.com/media/cache/resolve/728/files/chrome/images/201509/14/7ab25d35dab8db79e3be6507f6090896.png [Accessed 15 Apr. 2016].

Beks, A. (n.d.). Vaporwave is not dead. *The Essential*. Available at: http://theessential.com.au/features/the-catch-up/vaporwave-is-not-dead-nmesh-dream-sequins [Accessed 15 Apr. 2016].

Bérubé, M. (2005). Introduction. In: M. Bérubé, ed., *The aesthetics of cultural studies*. Massachusetts: Blackwell, pp. 1-28.

Beverly, J. (2000). Pedagogy and subalternity: Mapping the limits of academic knowledge. In: R.G. Paulston, ed., *Social cartography: mapping ways of seeing social and educational change*. New York, NY & London, UK: Garland Publishing Inc, pp. 347-356.

The Eagles. (1976). *Hotel California* [LP]. Los Angeles: Asylum. 7E-1084.

ECO VIRTUAL. (2013). *ATMOSPHERES 第1*.

George, M. (1984). *Careless Whisper* [7" single]. New York: Colombia. Columbia / 44-05170.

Harper, A. (2012). 'I'm applauding them': Unpublished James Ferraro interview and review. *Rogue's Foam*, June 10. Available at: http://rougesfoam.blogspot.ca/2012/06/im-applauding-them-unpublished-james.html [Accessed 15 Apr. 2016].

Harper, A. (2012). Vaporwave and the pop-art of the virtual plaza. *Dummy Mag*, July 12. Available at: http://www.dummymag.com/Features/adam-harper-vaporwave [Accessed 15 Apr. 2016].

Hughes, L. (2016). S U N D A Y S C H O O L. *YouTube*. Available at: https://www.youtube.com/watch?v=rTfa-9aCTYg [Accessed 23 Jan. 2016].

Larryhazard. (n.d.). *The tragedy of existence.* Available at: http://orig12.deviantart.net/9d08/f/2013/364/e/0/the_tragedy_of_existence__by_larryhazard-d700giv.jpg [Accessed 15 Apr. 2016].

Jameson, F. (2003). The end of temporality. *Critical inquiry* 29:4, pp. 695-718.

Jameson, F. (1992). *The geopolitical aesthetic: Cinema and space in the world system.* Bloomington: Indiana University Press.

Jameson, F. (1991). *Postmodernism, or the cultural logic of late capitalism.* Durham: Duke University Press.

Karuari. (n.d.). *Vaporwave aesthetic.* Available at http://karuari.deviantart.com/art/Vaporwave-Aesthetic-536118542 [Accessed 15 Apr. 2016].

Kidmograph. (2016). *Driving till the end...* March 6. Available at: https://s-media-cache-ak0.pinimg.com/236x/c9/af/f5/c9aff5acc91689d6e95c70487ae39377.jpg [Accessed 15 Apr. 2016].

Lhooq, M. (2013). Is vaporwave the next seapunk? *THUMP.* 27 December. Available at: https://thump.vice.com/en_ca/article/is-vaporwave-the-next-seapunk [Accessed 15 Apr. 2016].

Macintosh Plus. (2011). *Floral Shoppe* [Cassette]. Lawrence: Beer On The Rug.

Massumi, B. (1995). The autonomy of affect. *Cultural critique* 31, pp. 83-109.

Massumi, B. (1998). Sensing the virtual, building the insensible. *Architectural design* 68(5/6), pp. 16-24.

McKim, J. (2009). Of microperception and micropolitics: an interview with Brian Massumi, 15 August 2008. *INFLEXtions: a journal for research-creations* No. 3, October 2009, pp. 1-20.

Povinelli, E. (2011). *Economies of abandonment: Social belonging and endurance in late liberalism.* Durham & London: Duke University Press.

Randomstuff. (2015). What the fuck is this aestethic anyway? *The Vapor Wave.* January 20. Available at: https://thevaporwave.wordpress.com/ [Accessed 15 Apr. 2016].

Shaviro, S. (2010). Post-cinematic affect: on Grace Jones, Boarding Gate and Southland Tales. *Film-philosophy* 14:1, pp. 1-102.

SYLLABUS. (2014). Memories On The Horizon. *July* [Cassette]. Pittsburgh: Business Casual.

Tally Jr., R.T. (2000). Jameson's project of cognitive mapping: a critical engagement. In: R.G. Paulston, ed., *Social cartography: mapping ways of seeing social and educational change*. New York, NY & London, UK: Garland Publishing Inc, pp. 399-416.

Twin Peaks, (1991). Episode 29. TV, ABC. June 10.

Vang, O. (2015). *vaporwave*. October 30. Available at: https://www.themebeta.com/media/cache/resolve/728/files/chrome/images/201510/30/96902490fb25aba6152ed4397b6d05b8.jpeg [Accessed 15 Apr. 2016].

Williams, R. (1977). *Marxism and literature*. Oxford & New York: Oxford University Press.

猫 シ Corp. (2014). *Palm Mall*. No Problema Tapes.

Gayl Jones, Barricaded Feeling and Unstately Black Life

~~~~~

Sarah Jane Cervenak
UNIVERSITY OF NORTH CAROLINA, GREENSBORO

In the first chapter of *The Intimacies of Four Continents* (2015), Lisa Lowe theorizes the racialized and sexualized violences and "forgettings" that forged the modern project of liberal humanism.[1] She argues that the Enlightenment (and post-Enlightenment) investment in possessive individualism, buttressed as it is by the racialized and sexualized terrors engendered by the fetish of private property, also bespeaks the (right to) "interiority of person" (28). In other words, having a (right to) private desire and life is never not a feature of being propertied. That is, to be at-home in the world at once elaborates dual affective registers; that of (unfettered) ownership on the one hand and being trespassed on the other.

Following Lowe, the stabilization of such feeling meant the forcible removal of racialized, sexualized, gendered, and classed others; life tossed aside in the very ambulations of its sanctioned expression with evictions registering as the sensorial terrors of unhomed worlds and unhomed flesh.

Questions linger as unsettled: What is at stake when one is always imagined to be trespassing on another's sense/feeling of being at home? How does that evoke an un/homed structure of feeling that resounds as unsheltered itself, vulnerable to the state's ongoing regulatory procedures of shutting up and shutting out?

Still, what if being unsheltered or shut out opened another door? What if such a door moved along with other fleeting middle grounds or lonely kitchen floors that undulate somewhere between power's material and affective gated communities on the one hand, and being forced out of them on the other? In her short story, "The Seige", author Gayl Jones offers the barricaded room as this middle place, one that ushers in feeling worlds that disaggregate private, emotional life from the securities engendered and sanctioned by the presumption of (self-)possession itself. These are fleeting self-intimacies possible even when your (always temporary) home is surrounded. Crucially too, these gateless feeling-worlds amble as unknowable even as they philosophize other self-relationalities in a "disowned world" (Williams 1992, p.181). That is, at once, in the barricaded room, following Fred Moten, "the theory and practice [and I would add, affectivity] of stateless social life" occurs even as the theorization itself nestles in the barricade (Moten 2014, p.62).

"The Seige" begins with the cold language of a police report.[2] "A twenty-two year old woman with a shotgun, barricaded in a room in Cleveland. A young woman with a cat, a shotgun, a cot, a table. They decided to not use teargas, but at night they turned off the electricity and the water" (Jones 1982, p 89). The voice that opens the story worries about that twenty-two year old's unsettledness, where being unsettled might have something to do with the convergence of the barricade, the gun, the cat, blackness, supposed mental illness, a cot, and a table. Where unsettledness is an armed assertion of ante-eviction: "Never being on the right side of the Atlantic is an unsettled feeling, the feeling of a thing that unsettles with others. It's a feeling, if you ride with it, that produces a certain distance from the settled, from those who determine themselves in space and time, who locate themselves in a determined history" (Moten and Harney 2013, p. 97).

The main character is unsettled. They worry about that.

Very soon though, that worry dissipates into the tough conjunction of the SWAT team's bullhorn's echo and the textures awaiting the barricaded one inside. While she chews on a raw onion, the cat drinks powdered milk. Small unavailable worlds hover next to those tastings.

She remembers him, that mushroom hunter and ethics professor she loved. They used to hunt together. Sweet memories of such gathering along with frying up onions and eggs flow into one of the room's corners even as the radio's nervous repeating of her name "Jean Zane" settles into (and calls for her eviction from) another corner.

Still.

"Where there are no words there is music. Where there's music there are no words" (Jones 1982, p 90). In a certain kind of way, the music shares an anti-evictional kinship with Jean's memories; the latter says and suggests something that those folks outside the barricaded room can never know. They don't how it feels to be the unstately one, that "crazy person" they describe on the radio, the one who feels too crowded by the world's different words for mushroom. The one who wants to be with the Brazilian tribe in those photos, the tribe that took that "secret contraceptive plant so they wouldn't bear more into such a world, into such horror" (Jones 1982, p. 91). She just wants to see their faces, but won't explain why when asked. The one she loved heard her discuss that tribe, her deep sadness for them, and the terrible irony of their despair in a world that serializes a desire to "Save the Canadian Geese" (Jones 1982, p. 91).

Shouts from the outside echo, all the while she moves in the loving hold of his touch, the feel of his tongue in her mouth. The tongue as this world's anchor and makeshift shelter, entering into an untranscribable communion with the prose of a raw onion.

> And so they sit on what he calls, after the Spanish poet, the 'tongue of the river'.
> 'But isn't the water itself the tongue, always moving. One of the strongest muscles they say, the tongue is.'
> 'I knew you weren't dumb,' he says.
> He gives her his tongue. Another kiss. She's never had such kisses. The best ones she's had. (Jones 1982, p. 92)

Moving along the oceanic rhythms of that kiss, in the mouth of the world, Jean remembers their romance, its textures and quills. The things he got mad about. That conversation where she told him the doctors said she had schizophrenia but chalked it up to "what they always say when they have no answers…I didn't harm people. I was just too withdrawn. I built my own world" (Jones 1982, p. 92). After this disclosure, she decides to step out into the world with him and look for mushrooms. To "come up" from "underground" (Jones 1982, p. 93).

Her stay there was short, "He knew it wasn't the right mushroom and he ate it anyway" (Jones 1982, p. 94). She couldn't follow him *there;* she went back underground, "Still somehow she feels she's to blame" (Jones 1982, p. 94). There, in the underground, in the "intramural" party (Williamson 2015, p. 97); only to her, the cat, the powdered milk, and the shotgun, she sits with that guilt, "crowded and confused" (Jones 1982, p. 94).

> If only she can stay there, just for a little longer.
>
> They come in wearing iron suits. She lets them take her gun. She holds onto the cat (the wrong way).
> 'What's your story, girl?' one of them asks.
> 'No call for all this,' says another.
> Because she is harmless, they take off their armor. Because she is harmless, she won't let them touch her. (Jones 1982, p. 94)

What would it mean to leave Jean alone? With her cat and onion in the underground, within the stateless ambit of the unmappable corner, the barricaded room, her own lightless city? What would it mean if life, like a mushroom, grew there, in that unowned place, the in/temperate clime, the "crowded and confused" (Jones 1982, p. 94) pasture, the un/recorded textures of lost kisses and pungent vegetables? This life refuses to settle, where settling means some already fraudulent (heteropatriarchal, colonialist, ableist and anti-black) notion of self-possession. Instead, it thrives in the unsettlable folds of someone who only wants to feel herself, even as space and time themselves stay borrowed.

I'm not sure there's any other way to conclude, or rather I can't claim that a conclusion hasn't already taken place, either in the fold of the onion or in the taste of his tongue in her mouth. Maybe, in that way, what Gayl Jones' "The Seige" announces is the inherent impropriety of interpretation in the face of the unstately, the former's tendency to settle that which already made its (always temporary, fleeting) home in the misrecognized holds of another way.

References

Jones, G. (1982). The Seige. *Callaloo.* No. 16, pp. 89-94.

Lowe, L. (2015). *The Intimacies of Four Continents.* Durham: Duke University Press.

Moten, F. and S. Harney (2013). *The Undercommons: Fugitive Planning and Black Study.* New York: Minor Compositions.

Moten, F. (2014). Notes on Passage (The New International of Sovereign Feelings). *Palimpsest: Women, Gender and The Black International,* 3 (1), pp. 51-74.

Williams, P. (1992). *The Alchemy of Race and Rights: Diary of a Law Professor.* Cambridge: Harvard University Press.

Williamson, T. (2015). In the Life: Black Women and Serial Murder. *Social Text,* 33 (1 122), pp. 95-114.

Endnotes

1. I wrote this piece as I was working with my friend and collaborator, Dr. J. Kameron Carter on another essay, "Black Ether." This essay is deeply influenced by our study together and by what I've learned from him. I want to acknowledge that the phrase "racialized and sexualized forgettings" also appears in "Black Ether." Kameron Carter, J and Cervenak, S.J. (2016). Black Ether. CR: The New Centennial Review: James Baldwin's Lives, 16 (2) pp.203-224.

2. A fellow participant in the Black Performance Theory working group (2015), Dr. Raj Chetty, mentioned that "The Seige's" opening read to him like a police report. I wanted to acknowledge the influence of our conversation about it here.

Multiple generated faces using FaceMachine
Randallbritten, 2014

Coding Intensive Movement with Technologies of Visibility

Alien Affects

~~~~~

Michael Lechuga
THE UNIVERSITY OF TEXAS AT EL PASO

This is an essay about how alienhood is made. Alienhood is a material, affective, and political condition of that is manufactured by the State's technologies of visibility. Immigration control in the US relies on enhanced technologies of perception to surveil the intensive movement differences (alien affects) of migrants to control their extensive movements—their flow. Alien affects are the micro-flows of intensity that when cast upon the surface of the State, glimmer with difference, augmenting the ways alien migrant bodies move into and across the surfaces of US statehood. This makes the process of alienation a political process that involves governance of migrating bodies through a multitude of technologies aimed at surveilling and controlling both citizen communities and non-citizen communities. This essay explores the relationship between extensive movement and intensive movement and what this relationship means in the context of affect studies. It also describes how State power is expressed through layers of articulable and visible expression that is distributed across landscapes of US statehood to control the flows of the bodies. Lastly, the essay invites those invested in affect studies to find more links between the fields of rhetoric and affect studies, to study the technological production of alienhood in our societies of control, and to consider what adopting a movement politics can offer that ascribing to an identity politics may not.

KEYWORDS

Alien Affects, Rhetorical Materialism, Migration Control, Technologies of Visibility, Movement

Those living along the border between México and the United States (US) might never see a physical, 2,000-mile long wall between the two nations. If there is a border wall, it will likely be a virtual wall. I say this for two reasons: first, the US has invested tens of billions of dollars in the latest surveillance technologies over the last three decades, to create a network of sensing devices to track the movements of migrants across that border (Office of the Inspector General, 2005; US Customs and Border Protection, 2015a). These include seismic sensors buried in the desert, infrared cameras mounted on Hum-Vs and Predator Drones, and biometric face scanners at ports of entry. With most of that technology already in place, a physical wall that spans 2,000 miles seems both redundant and unrealistic.

Second, deporting all migrants unauthorized to be in the country and building an impenetrable wall would have detrimental effects on the nation's economy. One study estimates that deporting all the undocumented migrants in the US would cost the government nearly $5 trillion in lost Gross Domestic Product (GPD), and an additional $900 billion in lost revenue in the form of tax and interest payments over 10 years (Edwards & Ortega, 2016). On the other hand, capturing migrants into cycles of control—like migrant apprehension, detention, deportation, and others (often operated by private contractors)—benefits the US both economically and politically. After migrants enter the landscape of citizenship without authorization, they are driven into exploitative labor or get swept into the State's (anti-)migration apparatus where they are scooped up, held in stagnating detention centers, then flushed out through deportation. The State's technologies of visibility, like drone surveillance, biometric databases, and the 'virtual border', make the intensive and extensive movements of migrants moving into and through our landscapes of citizenship more sensible, thus making migrants more vulnerable.

These movements, alien affects, are not inherent to any body. They are a product of state power expressed through a network of technological surveillance apparatuses cast onto a body and set upon the backdrop of dominant State-flows traversing a national terrain. Migration control in the US relies on enhanced technologies of perception to surveil the intensive movements of migrants, in order to more closely control their extensive movements. In other words, the process of alienation is a political process that involves governance of bodies through a multitude of technologies aimed at surveilling and controlling both migrant communities and citizen communities. The State asserts its power in this way to shape a terrain that cuts the flows of alien migrant bodies from the flow of citizenship in our society of control. In this essay, I explore the relationship between extensive movement and intensive movement, and what this relationship means in the context of affect studies. I describe how State power is expressed through layers of articulable and visible expression that is distributed across landscapes of US statehood, to control the flows of the bodies within its territory. The final section makes a case for studying the technological production of alienhood in our societies of control, and considers a movement politics (in lieu of an identity politics) that addresses difference through a lens of mobility and affect.

Alien Bodies, Migrant Movements, and Coding Control

Alienhood is a material, affective, and political condition of national non-belonging signaling difference to those moving with and against dominant flows on landscapes of relation. Alien affects are the felt intensities of magnitude, differences between a citizen body and a transnational migrant body that are illuminated by the State's technologies of visibility, as bodies move through the physical, social, and economic landscapes of the nation.[1] This essay is a description of the relationship between extensive and intensive movements of migrant bodies and the technologies of visibility used by the State to surveil them and code them as alien. Here, the term alien is both a political and an economic expression. In the political sense, the alien is the barbaric, foreign Other that lives beyond the walls of the *polis* (Nail 2015, p.52). It emerges as a nationalist figure; it is the opposite of a citizen. In an economic sense, the alien is capital's exploited laborer. Thinking about today's low-wage, unauthorized migrants from México, Central America, and Asia living in the US, the political and economic contexts of alienhood are one and the same.

Alien Affects

Alien affects are intensive movements of national difference that shimmer on an individual body as it encounters the State's technologies of visibility on a national plane. They are perceivable tonal differences—like an accent, a glance, or maybe just a feeling that something is off—that vary from the dominant flows of citizenship circulating throughout the terrain of the State. They shape the relationships among bodies moving through those terrains. In the US, for example, the aural alien affects that are noticeable in non-native American English speakers to Native American English speakers is off. The tonal differences in a non-native speaker's voice signals national difference in the listener and likely shapes the relationships between native and non-native language speakers. This example demonstrates how intensive movements (like vocal variations) can affect extensive movements (how foreigners might move through a community depending on how welcoming they are to foreigners).

For Gilles Deleuze and Felix Guattari (1987), extensive movement is what we generally conceive of today as movement; it is movement from one place to another over a given span of distance and over time: "[It] designates the relative character of a body considered as 'one,' and which goes from point to point" (p. 381). This type of movement, movement as we classically understand it, is usually divided from the realm of the intensive mostly because it constitutes the realm of the perceivable (and eventually measurable) (De Landa, 2002). Extensive movement is locomotion; it is movement from point A to point B.

Intensive movement, what Deleuze and Guattari call speed (velocity), on the other hand, is that felt qualitative difference that "constitutes the absolute character of a body " (author's emphasis, 1988, p. 381). Speed is intensive; it is qualitative movement; it is vibrational, affective, and always in-becoming. Unlike the external logic of "the one," it is the internal logic of relationality and deindividuation (Manning, 2007 & 2011). A body perceives intensive movement by "feel[ing] that the quality perceived analyses itself into repeated and successive vibrations, bound together by an inner continuity" (Bergson 1911, p. 269). Felt intensive movement always occurs as a sense of qualitative difference; it is active and continuous change (Bergson, 1911). Intensive movement is qualitative change or tone; it is a shift in the intensity of a felt affect. Migrants' extensive movement is typically the focus of migrant control in public discourse, in border crossing for example.

However, the figure of the transnational migrant is simultaneously a nomadic body that is moving from fixed point to point, and also a national figure "affect[ing] an intensive or qualitative social movement of the whole of society ... the figure of the migrant is a socially constitutive power. It is the subjective figure that allows society to move and change" (Nail 2015, p. 13). One study recently discussed how fewer white babies were born in the US (49.8%), than babies that "racial or ethnic minorities" (50.2%). For many (in white communities), this number signals a societal shift and creates anxiety over foreigners (Cohn, 2016). Studies like this one demonstrate Nail's point that the migrants body and its intensive movements affect the relationships of those in a national landscape.

Intensive and extensive movements are not separate types of movements; they are parts of the same universe of flow that are only sensed on different criteria—qualitatively and quantifiably. After all, being "is an intensive quality, as if each one of us were defined by a kind of complex of intensities which refers to her/his essence, and also of relations which regulate the extended parts, the extensive parts" (Deleuze 1978, p. 12). The relations of bodies and their extensive mobility in each landscape affect and are affected by the complex of felt intensities attached to each body. This is key in making sense of how the relationship between intensive and extensive might be governed. Should those operating today's control societies develop an ability to modulate any or all the intensities that make up a body's complex of intensities, they may very well be able to shape the extensive movements of bodies. Most everyone has a unique complex of intensive movements that are perceived differently in different landscapes (Brennan, 2004). If it benefits a society (of control) to control the extensive movements of the bodies that are moving through the national landscapes, then those societies might begin policing the intensive movements of those bodies.

The State apparatus in the US today is heavily invested in both strengthening dominant national (cultural, economic, and even genetic) flows, and capturing migrant flows into cycles of violence, exploitation, and expulsion. Those bodies that easily move with dominant national flows have low-magnitude intensive movements. In comparison to dominant intensive flows—like light skin color (a visual intensity of light waves), American English accent (an aural intensity of sound waves), and other qualitative cues—these bodies do not vary from the norm. There is nothing in their complexes of intensities that is resistant to the dominant flows of the US; they are low-magnitude in relation to desired State flows. Those with high-magnitude intensive movements, on the other hand, project intensive difference when cast upon the landscape of dominant US American flows. These intensities are high-magnitude because they are noticeably incongruent with the dominant felt intensities that populate a nation. For example, cues like a person's skin color, eye color, face shape, accent, smell, posture, gate, or even touch can signal alienhood to others. These qualitative intensities of national non-belonging that are perceived in political terrains of relation are alien affects.

The process of producing alien affects is a movement-centered political division. Those with low-magnitude intensive movements easily move (extensively) through national landscapes—across highways, over borders, in and out of public view—with little to no resistance. On the contrary, bodies with high-magnitude intensive movement are unable to easily move through cities or cross international borders without at least some resistance from State agents. Sheriff Joe Arpaio of Maricopa County, AZ, for example, was a proponent of racial profiling law AZ

SB 1070 which allowed state law enforcement to stop and arrest individual who looked Mexican, regardless of her or his citizenship (Santos 2016). On an interpersonal level, we can see how the perception of alien affects by some in the US leads to the rejection and mistreatment of migrants in their own community. In 2014, when Alabama passed HB 56—also known as the "self-deportation" bill—many migrants reported that they were being ignored, shamed, or even verbally assaulted by members of their communities for simply being migrants (Lechuga 2015). Collectively, these expressions can drive migrants away from unfriendly spaces and into the shadows of society.

At the State level, migrant groups remain the most vulnerable to control; those with alien affects are likely to be captured in cycles of economic exploitation, targeted and apprehended by law-enforcement, placed in detention, and flushed out through deportation infrastructure. The State can multiply its social, economic, and political power through the capture, exploitation, and expulsion of low-skilled, low-wage labor—mostly from México, Central America, and Asia: "When societies desire change or expansion, they may harness the mobility of the migrant in the form of slavery, militarism, incarceration, and waged labor in order to help them expand" (Nail 2015, p. 14). The corporatized State uses this group of expendable bodies to fill seasonal, low-skill labor demands, to meet the quotas set for migrant detention and deportation infrastructure, and to serve as a political scapegoat for the rightists.

To power the anti-migrant flows, the State relies on bordering apparatuses like ports of entry, highway checkpoints, racial profiling, biometric databases, and others to drive those with alien affects into exploitation and removal. These processes are materially shaping a national terrain in the US to divide citizens from aliens: "The internal vocation of state politics is the unification of aims and the organization of those aspirations into a unique spatiotemporal whole" (Manning 2007, p. 62). Bodies of migrants, citizens, and others are plugged into systems of relation that are distributed throughout the landscapes of the State for the purposes of placing migrant bodies into apparatuses that maximize the state's political power over them. Bodies shimmering with alien affects flow across landscapes of citizenship differently than low-magnitude bodies. By producing (illuminating and coding) more highly-intense aliens, the State's widespread migrant surveillance systems unevenly contour landscapes of citizenship and further shape the movements of migrants moving through them. The techno-militarized state apparatuses of surveillance, apprehension, and removal are distributed across the spatiotemporal landscapes that make up the spaces of citizenship in the US—both at the border between México and the US and the throughout the national landscape—to produce these highly intensive aliens.

Illuminating and Coding Alien Affects

The division of migrant flows from the dominant flows of citizenship occurs at the moment alien affects are sensed by those in relation to migrating bodies. So, the US State citizenship apparatus has heavily invested in technologies of visibility that make alien affects more easily sensed by others. For example, the ground sensors in the New Mexico desert and the infrared cameras attached to US Customs and Border Protection (CBP) drones surveil the edges of the national terrain to detect the movements (both extensive and intensive) of migrants. Then, these movements are coded and digitally transmitted to border agents who become aware of the migrant movements. This usually results in the mobilization of other border agents who attempt to apprehend the migrants (Lechuga 2016, p. 156). The evolution of technologies of visibility for migration control—from the systems of lights in the 1980s and 1990s to today's hi-tech network of border surveillance equipment—has allowed the State to more easily surveil the paths migrants take into the United States' terrain, capture them, and channel them into violent cycles of control. After all, "visibility is a trap" (Foucault 1977, p. 200).

In disciplinary societies, technologies of visibility are just as vital to erecting diagrams of State power on the bodies within the institution as the institution itself (Chow, 2010; Deleuze, 1988).

> Foucault associated the process of making-visible with an intensifying order of collectively enforced aggression against the human individual. Light … is theorised by Foucault not as a medium of emancipation but explicitly as a medium of entrapment: precisely as it enables one to be seen, it also enables one to be caught (Chow 2010, p. 67)

Articulable and visible State power is dispersed over open surfaces of statehood in today's societies of control by diagrams of power, or systems of governing apparatuses: "Visibilities are not to be confused with elements that are visible, or more generally perceptible, such as qualities, things, objects, compounds of objects … visibilities are not forms of objects, nor even forms that would show up under light, but rather forms of luminosity which are created by the light itself and allow a thing or object to exist as a flash, sparkle or shimmer" (Deleuze 1988, p. 52). These apparatuses govern "the relations between forces (visible and articulable) unique to a particular formation, [they are] the distribution of the power to affect and the power to be affected" (Deleuze 1988, p. 72–73). However, where technologies of visibility that once illuminated bodies captured in the institutions of Foucault's disciplinary society, they are now cast onto all the bodies freely (and not so freely), flowing through Deleuze's societies of control.

By disbursing the technologies of visibility that make migrant bodies sensible to others, for example, the State can cast a layer of articulable anti-immigration law onto a body of a person who moves (both intensively and extensively) differently than other bodies in this landscape of citizenship. Technologies like floodlights, ground sensors, night vision, closed circuit television cameras, and even news cameras all produce a visible migrant body that is moving across the surface of citizenship, not necessarily confined within the institutions of State control (yet). In making migrants more visible through traditional and technologically advanced surveillance, bordering agents are often able to apprehend these migrants more easily, taking them off their nomadic extensive flow and corralling them into detention facilities, where they might sit for years without a trial, or worse, be deported with no chance to appeal for asylum (Martin & Yankay 2014). This process is not new, though; it has been the logic of migrant control for decades. With advancements in surveillance and biometric technologies, though, the State is now relying more and more on the coding of intensive alien affects to make them shimmer with alienhood.

Nearly all bodies are illuminated by the optical mechanisms of citizenship control that are mobilized throughout our national landscapes. Think, for example, about the more the 70 permanent Border Patrol checkpoints that are distributed throughout the US Southwest. In disciplinary societies, the apparatuses of enclosure "are first and foremost places of visibility dispersed in a form of exteriority, which refer back to an extrinsic function, that of setting apart and controlling" (Deleuze 1988, p. 60). Technologies of light in these apparatuses are used to surveil and control the entirety of the landscape of the State by illuminating those individuals visibly marked with alienhood—differing extensive and intensive movements. In control societies, while light is useful to illuminate extensive movement, coding illuminates intensive movement: "The digital language of control is made up of codes indicating whether access to some information should be allowed or denied" (Deleuze 1995, p. 180). This includes access to certain spaces on the surface of citizenship. Thus, technologies of visibility have evolved from a discipline logic lighting and capturing bodies, to a control logic that codes and modulates the flows of bodies. Alien migrants, for example, are now illuminated on national surfaces using technologies, like infrared cameras and/or facial recognition devices, that digitally code their alien affects as the emerge in the low-intensity flows of US statehood.

To make sense of coding, begin with the assumption that bodies are complexes of energy flows (Deleuze 1988; Massumi 2015). Bodies are culminations of waves and forces and frequencies: "The small-scale (in)dividuals populating the [control society] are themselves populated by coexisting metastable states" (Massumi 2015, p. 40). The "dividual" is no longer the product of an institutional mold or caste, like the graduate from school or a rehabilitated patient that emerges from the asylum, but is the amalgamation of myriad frequencies that are simultaneously in tune with innumerable flows within the economic, cultural, political, national, and other currents in the State (Deleuze 1995; Massumi 2015). Deleuze describes how bodies move through the innumerable flows of consumer-statehood as a kind of "surfing", "undulat[ing], moving among a continuous range of different orbits" (Deleuze 1995, p. 180). Alien bodies, thus, are often coded as such through a specific affective "metastable state"—alien affect—made perceivable by technologies of State visibility (including visual media like news reporting). These technologies illuminate the alien affect, code the body as alien, and trap the body in an orbit around state apparatuses of control.

Take for example, the use of facial recognition software used at ports of entry. These facial scanners, installed by CBP in 2012, are keeping a digital database of thousands of migrants who regularly enter and leave the country (Sternstein 2015). This technology casts a light onto the face of the migrant then captures a digital image of the face. The image is coded using specific relationships between features of the person's face—a series of intensive movements—and then stored in CPB databases to track the exit and reentry of migrants crossing US borders. Should a migrant be caught without authorization for entry, or be suspected of criminal activity, they can be detained or denied entry, even at US airports. This example shows how illuminating and coding the intensive movements of migrants allows the State to surveil and control their extensive movements. With advancements in technologies, like digital photography, digital video, data management, drone surveillance, and others, the State can more easily manufacture alienhood that has a lasting residual effect on those who encounter alien affects.

Aliens, both transnational and intergalactic extraterrestrials that are seen in Hollywood cinema, for example, are bodies with several foreign qualitative intensities (and many likely not so foreign). Migrant and extraterrestrial bodies shimmering with alien affects are noticeable on today's landscapes of citizenship precisely because when they are cast upon the low-intensity national flow, the qualitative movements of intensity that are coded as alien are lit up by technologies of visibility. For example, border surveillance technology like infrared cameras and night vision are used by the US CBP along the border capture migrant aliens by focusing on their heat signature—intensive movements made apparent by the technology. These images, digitized and transmitted via the CPB data network are distributed to border agents who see the thermal reading and mobilize to apprehend potential unauthorized migrants. Since these are digital technologies, they rely on a digital coding to make sense of the data and mobilize a response. Thus, aliens are sensed by the technologies, coded as alien moving across national surfaces, and quickly apprehended and channeled into cycles of State violence. The improvements in bordering technology had been a "force multiplier" for the State (US Customs and Border Protection, 2015b).

We can see this process in the cinematic construction of alienhood as well. Technologies of visibility, both traditional (lights and cameras), and digital (CGI), make highly intense aliens visible on cinematic landscapes, then mobilize the military to capture and expel the alien. Elsewhere, I suggest that the process of making alien affects felt on geographical landscapes, cinematic landscapes, and many others relies on coding technologies of visibility (Lechuga 2016, p. 104). On geographic surfaces, they illuminate both the extensive movements (nomadic in their trajectory), and code the intensive movements of migrants (alien affects), moving through border spaces. On screen, they give us enormous, grotesque, slimy, and dangerous extraterrestrial invaders with a combination of traditional cinematography (lighting), and CGI (coding). It should be no surprise that the same companies that are developing imaging technologies for the militarized border security apparatus are the same ones working with Hollywood to produce the highly intense images of extraterrestrial aliens in popular cinema.4 Over time and as the technologies of visibility improve, alienhood will likely become more intense, and the dominant flow of US nationhood will likely strengthen. The flows of resources and technologies between the State governing apparatuses, the military bordering apparatuses, cinematic apparatuses, and many others are also likely to strengthen, further modulating the flows of both visible and articulable power.

Trajectories

Manufacturing alienhood is a political act. It is one way the State expresses its power over the surfaces of citizenship in the US. The State military-industrial-legal-cinematic (-and-probably-more) complex is distributing technologies of visibility to make alienhood more noticeable, to capture those with alien affects. The dominant national flows of citizenship in the US continue to intensify, evidenced by the election of an isolationist government, the increase in Immigration and Customs Enforcement (ICE) raids, and the funding of a border wall (which I still think will be a digital wall). Much still must be done to illuminate just how violent and exploitative migrant control in the US has become.

This leads me to consider three trajectories for further research on migration in societies of control. First, technologies of visibility exist in a world also populated by mediated symbols. As demonstrated by Deleuze writing on Foucault, the articulable and visible (sensible), are one in the same expression of power. They are inseparable from each other. Ronald Greene's rhetorical materialism, for example, offers those interested in the avenues between the two fields a way to conceptualize how rhetorical power is moved through governing apparatuses to subjugate and control bodies. This approach can map how power is "transformed, displaced, deployed and/or challenged by a particular governing apparatus … for the purpose of policing a population" (Greene 1998, p. 39). Rhetorical materialism, is "committed to mapping the ways bodies affect and are affected by rhetorical techniques and technologies [that] compose organizations of power" (Bost & Greene, 2011, p. 444). In this sense, by studying technologies of visibility, one might find ways that governing organizations compose themselves to enact State power.

Second, there is a material flow of resources, bodies, technologies, and other mechanisms that are being controlled to multiply State power. Studying alien affects—and other examples of the ways technologies of visibility are utilized to control bodies within State spaces—from an orientation toward affects studies, questions the ways our "dividuated" intensities are surveilled and controlled. By doing so, the State apparatuses can modulate the ways our bodies flow through spaces of statehood. By controlling those intensive movements of bodies, States can accelerate the mobility for some bodies on certain terrains of relation while making it difficult for others to easily move about. Making sense of the relationship between intensive and extensive movements can provide a great deal of insight to the ways bodies are controlled by the State. In addition to studying this relationship, scholarship is needed on the industrial influences on the governing apparatuses used by the State to modulate the flows of nationhood.

Finally, some bodies move differently than others. Many of those bodies in the US today move in ways that are not in rhythm with the State's consumer, political, and social flows. Therefore, a study of citizenship control, alien affects, class division, gender discrimination, ableism, or other studies of political division should move away from an identity politics and toward, what I suggest is, a movement politics. While identity politics can often be a critical methodological approach that challenges the State, it often falls back onto an inclusion/exclusion dynamic. Identity politics can rely on the same political, social, and economic subjectivities that are constituted by State or corporate interests; meaning the State's power still has primacy in its ability to subject a body in the first place, regardless of the relationship between those subjected groups. A movement politics, on the other hand, rejects in-group/out-group subjections of the State and focuses on making sense of the ways bodies' intensive and extensive movements affect their mobility in landscapes of belonging. It activates identity politics with a quality of motion. It can make sense of how power is moved through us and we are moved by power to form "relationscapes" of division (Manning 2013, p.102). Movement politics understands that the cultural construction of identity is a culmination of our intensive and extensive movements. We are (becoming) who we are (becoming) because of how are we moving. In this sense, we are each migrants who are constantly moving from one place (or "metastable state"), to another.

Endnotes

1. The term I use, 'alien affects', is different from Sarah Ahmed's (2010) notion of affect aliens. She describes an affect alien as one who's affection resists the expected emotional communication for a given interaction. Like the kill joy, the affect alien makes others feel something other than what should be felt (Ahmed 2010). This differs from my discussion of alien affects for two main reasons. first, alien affects are shimmers that are produced by state technologies that are cast upon bodies. What is created is a set of affective intensities, when set upon the backdrop of dominant state flows, that shimmer with alienhood. Second, alien affects are made up of a few intensities within the multitude of a body's multitude of intensities, while the affect alien is a subjectivity belonging to an individual.

References

Ahmed, S. (2010). *The Promise of Happiness.* Durham, NC: Duke University Press.

Bauman, Z. (1998). *Globalization: The Human Consequences.* New York: Columbia University Press.

Bergson, H. (1911). *Matter and Memory.* Translated by N. M. Paul and S. Palmer. New York: MacMillan Company.

Bost, M. & Greene, R. W. (2011). Affirming Rhetorical Materialism: Enfolding the Virtual and the Actual. *Western Journal Communication*, 75(4), 440–444.

Brennan, T. (2004). *The Transmission of Affect.* Ithica, NY: Cornell University Press.

Caluya, G. (2010). The Post-Panoptic Society? Reassessing Foucault in Surveillance Studies. *Social Identities*, 16(5), 621–33.

Chow, R. (2010). Postcolonial Visibilities: Questions Inspired by Deleuze's Method. In S. Bignall and P. Patton, eds. *Deleuze and the Postcolonial.* Edinburgh: Edinburgh University Press, pp. 62–77.

Cohn, D. (2016, 23 June). It's official: Minority babies are the majority among the nation's infants, but only just [online]. *Pew Research Institute.* Available at http://www.pewresearch.org/fact-tank/2016/06/23/its-official-minority-babies-are-the-majority-among-the-nations-infants-but-only-just/

De Landa, M. (2002). *Intensive Science & Virtual Philosophy.* New York: Bloomsbury.

Deleuze, G. (1978). Lecture Transcripts on Spinoza's Concept of Affect. [online] *Les Cours de Gilles Deleuze.* Available at http://www.gold.ac.uk/media/images-by-section/departments/research-centres-and-units/research-centres/centre-for-invention-and-social-process/deleuze_spinoza_affect.pdf [Accessed 19 Feb. 2017].

Deleuze, G. (1988). *Foucault.* Translated by S. Hand. Minneapolis: University of Minnesota Press.

Deleuze, G. (1995). *Negotiations.* Translated by M. Joughin. New York: Columbia University Press. (Original work published 1990).

Deleuze, G. and Guattari, F. (1987). *A Thousand Plateaus: Capitalism and Schizophrenia.* Translated by B. Massumi. Minneapolis: University of Minnesota Press.

Edwards, R. & Ortega, F. (2016, 21 September). The Economic Impacts of Removing Unauthorized Immigrant Workers. [online] *Center for American Progress*. Available at https://www.americanprogress.org/issues/immigration/reports/2016/09/21/144363/the-economic-impacts-of-removing-unauthorized-immigrant-workers/ [Accessed 21 Feb. 2017].

Greene, R. W. (1998). Another materialist rhetoric. *Critical Studies in Mass Communication*, 15(1), pp. 21–41.

Lash, S. (2010). *Intensive Culture: Social Theory, Religion & Contemporary Capitalism*. Thousand Oaks, CA: SAGE Publications.

Lechuga, M. (2014). Alien Affects: Movement, Migration, and Landscapes of Citizenship [Dissertation]. [Online] Available at http://digitalcommons.du.edu/etd/1132/.

Lechuga, M. (2014). Affective boundaries in a landscape of shame: Writing HB 56. *Journal of Argumentation in Context*. 3(1), pp. 83–101.

Manning, E. (2007). *Politics of Touch: Sense, Movement, Sovereignty.* Minneapolis, MN: University of Minnesota Press.

Manning, E. (2009). *Relationscapes: Movement, Art, Philosophy*. Cambridge, MA: MIT Press.

Martin, D. C. and Yankay, J. E. (2014, August). Refugees and Asylees: 2013. [online] *U.S. Department of Homeland Security*. Office of Immigration Statistics, Annual Flow Report. Available at http://www.dhs.gov/sites/default/files/publications/ois_rfa_fr_2013.pdf [Accessed 12 Jan. 2017)

Massumi, B. (1995). The Autonomy of Affect. *Cultural Critique*, 31, The Politics of Systems and Environments, Part II, pp. 83–109.

Massumi, B. (2015). *The Power at the End of the Economy*. Durham, NC: Duke University Press.

Nail, T. (2013). The Crossroads of Power: Michel Foucault and the US/Mexico Border Wall. *Foucault Studies*, 15, pp. 110–128.

Nail, T. (2015). *The Figure of the Migrant*. Stanford, CA: Stanford University Press.

Office of Inspector General (2005). A Review of Remote Technology along U.S. Land Borders. [online] *Department of Homeland Security*. Available at https://www.oig.dhs.gov/assets/Mgmt/OIG_06-15_Dec05.pdf [Accessed 19 Feb. 2017].

Santos, F. (2016, 15 September). Arizona limits police actions in enforcing immigration law [online]. *New York Times*. Available at https://www.nytimes.com/2016/09/16/us/arizona-limits-police-enforce-immigration.html?_r=0

Sternstein, A. (2015, 28 January). Homeland Security to roll out biometrics along the border this summer [online]. *Defense One*. Available at http://www.defenseone.com/technology/2015/01/homeland-security-roll-out-biometrics-along-border-summer/103968/

United States Customs and Border Protection (2015 a). Border patrol history. [online] *Department of Homeland Security*. Available at http://www.cbp.gov/border-security/along-us-borders/history [Accessed 5 Feb. 2017].

United States Customs and Border Protection (2015 b). Border security: At ports of entry [online]. Available at http://www.cbp.gov/border-security/ports-entry [Accessed 11 May 2017].

Whitehead, A. N. (1967). *Adventures of Ideas*. New York: The Macmillan Company.

Strange Air

Mathew Arthur
VANCOUVER SCHOOL OF THEOLOGY

[Tokens], Mathew Arthur, 2012

Three in the morning, our driver veers through the never-empty streets. Dodging potholes and stray freight trucks. The old city, a flashing light, the new city. A radio tower, the city under-construction, the colonial city, ruins, poverty, commerce, dust, luxury, uneven paving stones, an ocher moon, a howl, police sirens. Exhaust hangs thick in the air. An hour earlier, we were thirty-thousand feet up, circling, waiting to land, suspended by a gust of wind in an upholstered metal fuselage. In the recycled air of a dim economy-class cabin, from the wet air of home to the ozone-polluted air (now) of this sprawling valley, breath threads an invisible line. Air pervades. Smell, dirt, thickness, a metallic taste, aching lungs. Smog is ozone, an irritant that sears my airways, causes my lungs—invisible—to swell and redden. Invisible, air enters my body as sensation.

Air is habitat, each cubic metre filled with hundreds of micro-organisms (Womack et al 2010). "Air is messy," a space of encounter across scales, between species and lives, between life and not-life (Bakke 2011, p. 1). And the space of air is everywhere and nowhere—a space of entanglement. Air is imprecise. A faint scent, a draft, stale, salty, oppressive, alive and life-giving, wet, endless, hanging. No matter how heavy or thick its presence, air has no form or weight. Yet it persists in leaving an impression; the surface of water "translates air as texture" (McKay 2013, p. 13). Poisoned lungs, a turbine, a cyclone-wasted suburb, the leaves of a shaking aspen. Air transforms. Leaves its mark. As we weave through the nighttime streets, the air hangs sullen and paints our nostrils with yellow dust. We breathe with the city (particulate, metal, gas, poison, dander, creature, stranger) inside of us.

Apprehending breath with wonder renders air strange. Breathing opens a body to what is radically other, inhaling and exhaling "others and self and others-in-self-as-other" (Rubenstein 2008, p. 189). Body and air come together in breath to animate and disperse a self. To breathe as a body open to the world is a self-less suffering of wonder and uncertainty (p. 195). To breathe in and out this way is to remain vulnerable and porous, to respire words—old, new, silent, ancestral, absent, or imagined—that open worlds to possibility. To stand in wonder, in breath, inhale-exhale, is to give way to adoration. This world, our world, is adoration. A world radically open to itself, only, and nothing more. Adoration is modulated by breath, in breathing with a world. Bodies are "adoration in all their openings" (Nancy 2013, p. 20).

In the old city, we work our way through the crowded market stalls. Vendors sell bulk foodstuffs, tobacco, housewares, and counterfeit shoes, DVDs, eyewear, or wristwatches. Winding, kilometre-long aisles suspend and reverse time: colour, style, brand, scent, desire, greed, plastic, metal, texture, noise, symbol, mess. Capitalism, whatever (and wherever) it is, abstracts. It feigns authenticity, grit, reward, or nostalgia. In the thrum of the market, time stands still as if set in a resin of air. We hold our breath and clutch our pockets. We want, we charm, we transact and collect. This is the trick of capitalism: to render familiarity and meaning without contingence, as if out of time, out of breath. But isn't time, real time, heterogeneous—alive like the habitat of air? Like breath, the manifold of time transforms and reconfigures relations (Sewell 2008, p. 15). So, we stop to breathe. Now, the crowded stalls and rows of acid colour lurch as symptoms of desperation, class, extraction, displacement, opportunity, toxicity, alienation, success, comfort, and disease. We see the passing of time as both ecstasy and destruction: a gash in the land, beauty, deforestation, safety, pollution, the absence of hunger, warmth, or a ravaged landscape with ever-expanding edges. We breathe and feel god-like, apocalyptic, humble.

Experience includes both the "normal" timespace of the everyday—but also moments when "something elemental breaks into consciousness" (Fishbane 2008, p. 20-33). The caesural event invades the mundane and demands an attention to worldly contingence. To breathe with wonder is to disrupt the everyday, to disrupt the fixity of inheritances and creeds, and to disrupt the sly calm of a self in its capitalist temporality. In the act of breathing, neuronal pathways are synchronized: taste, touch, and smell are connected to perception and memory only through the breath, though the air (Lieff 2010). To know the world is to breathe with the world, to loosen or make-wide the self, to disperse, to let go, to gasp—exasperated—and, in the act of letting go, become air.

[Tokens], Mathew Arthur, 2012

References

Bakke, M. (2011). *The Life of Air: Dwelling, Communicating, Manipulating.* London: Open Humanities Press.

Fishbane, M. (2008). *Sacred Attunement: A Jewish Theology.* Chicago: University of Chicago Press.

Lieff, J. (2010). Breathing Alters Perception [online]. Available at: http://jonlieffmd.com/blog/breathing-alters-perception [Accessed 11 May 2017].

Mckay, D. (2013). *Strike/Slip.* Toronto: McClelland & Stewart.

Nancy, J.-L. (2013). *Adoration: The Deconstruction of Christianity II,* trans. John McKeane. New York: Fordham University Press.

Rubenstein, M.-J. (2008). *Strange Wonder: The Closure of Metaphysics and the Opening of Awe.* New York: Columbia University Press.

Sewell, W. (2008). The Temporalities of Capitalism. *Socio-Economic Review* 6 (3), p. 517-537.

Womack, A., Bohannan B., and Green, J. (2010). Biodiversity and Biogeography of the Atmosphere, Philosophical Transactions of the Royal Society of London, Series B. *Biological Sciences* 365 (1558), pp. 3645-53.

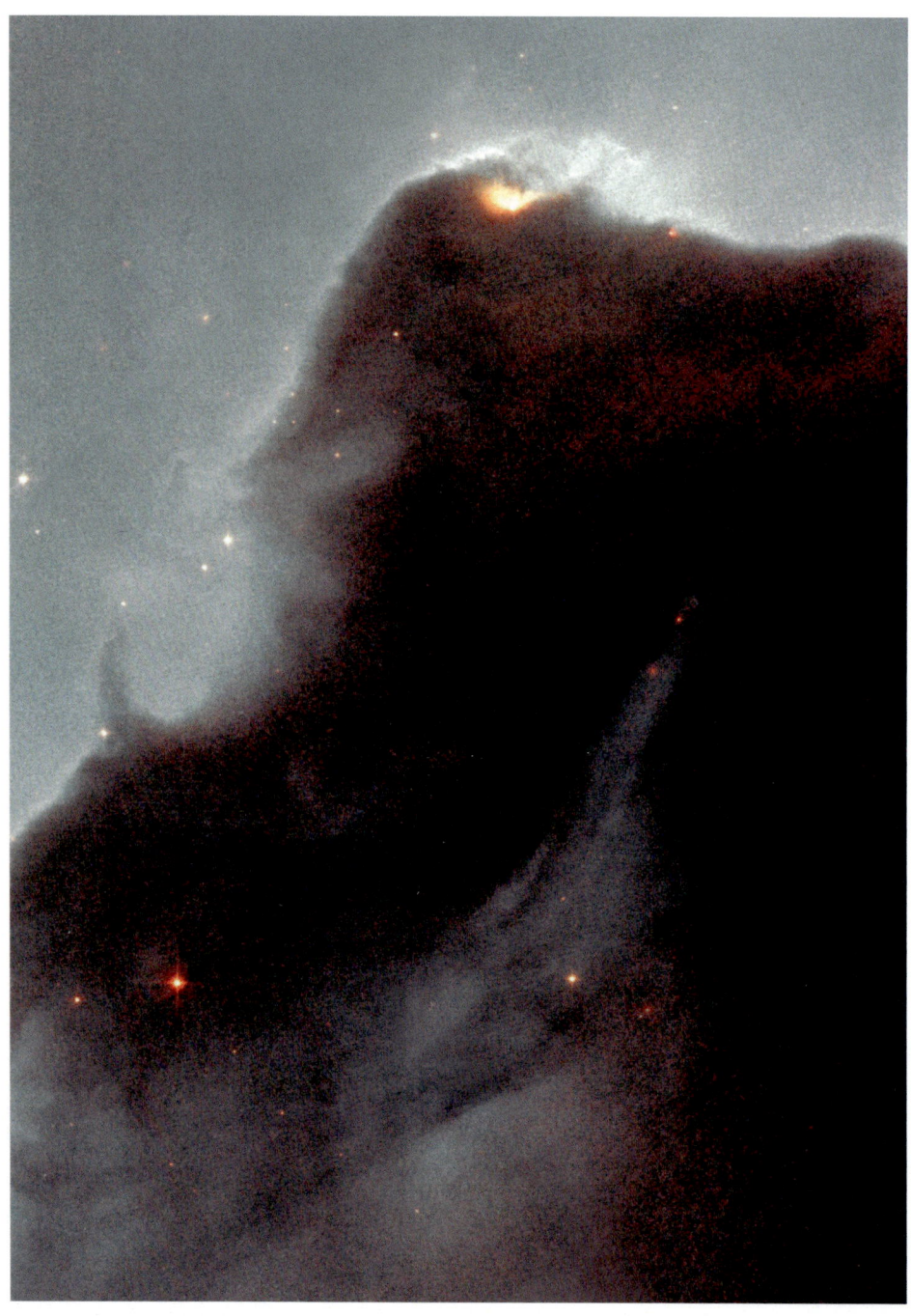

Infrared photograph of Horsehead Nebula
NASA/ESA/Hubble Heritage Team, 2012

When Dust Gets in Your Eyes

Researching the Taboo

~~~~~

Fiona Murray
UNIVERSITY OF EDINBURGH

This paper has emerged out of a black cloud which disseminates dust and soot more than epistemic knowledge. How do we talk into our research topics when soil folds in to the crevices of our trachea and the earth is in our eyes? How do we embrace a speculative pragmatism in order to stay with the processual and the more-than and avoid making a priori decisions? And what if we find ourselves during this process to be thinking with the taboo, thinking in the act (Erin Manning and Brian Massumi, 2014) with the grime that has tangled in our hair? This paper examines how affect theory puts the political firmly on the table.

KEYWORDS
Pornography, Affect, Taboo

Email Exchange

OUTGOING

Dear Mark,

Just checking that we are good for June. I'm really looking forward to coming to visit and to meet some other students and hearing about their research.

All Best,

Fiona

INCOMING

Hi Fiona,

Good to hear from you. Yes, looking forward to it. Will you also talk a little about your research?

Cheers,

Mark

Hi Mark,

Yes, absolutely. I'd love to. I've made a couple of short films that I could show, some special effects which aim to convey an autistic perception of the world. I would love to hear how the films work on others. I haven't shown them to anybody yet. But, I guess I should also say that there are a couple of fleeting but explicit sex scenes in them, just in the background, in the distance, not at too close proximity. It sounds more ominous than it is but I'd rather people knew that before they came. I hope that won't put anyone off. . .

Fiona

Mark does not come back to me for a while.

Four years earlier

Agitation fermented in the university classroom as I was asked to enunciate my initial ideas for a research topic. The root of this fermentation was not an issue of having a lack of ideas because as Elizabeth Grosz says, "ideas follow one another in rapid succession, largely but not solely dependent on the flow of the perception of objects" (2017, p. 77). Neither was the agitation around not wanting to commit. Far from it. My angst was such that I was more than ready to launch in and claim a mission as my own. My perceived 'problem' was that I was still inhabiting the 'dissolve' that Stacy Alaimo explains to be where "fundamental boundaries have begun to become undone, unravelled by unknown futures" (2016, p. 2), or that I was perhaps embracing an autistic perspective. This neurodiverse perspective, when entered into from the side and at the angle of speciation as opposed to pathology, is possible for all (Massumi, 2013). Donna Williams describes autistic perspective as a feeling which "comes from a time before words, before thought, before interpretation, before competition, before reliance on the conscious mind and before identity, in a time where all new experiences are equal in their worth and there is, as yet, no discrimination and no established sense of boundaries or hierarchy" (1998, p. 12). The circling agitation in the classroom for me was around notions of external pressures to verbalise my topic which at this point, had not yet tuned to language (Manning, p. 2016). For me to have attempted to shape my project by my own volition, to not wait for incipiency to become directionality (Manning, 2016), would have been for me to interrupt process and in so doing, unwittingly side-step the particular politics of my project.

How can I work to conceptualise my research whilst working with new modes of expression that curtail any *a priori* decision-making? After all, it is in this space of coming-to-be, where the problem is intuited from within, that a rigor of experimentation emerges (Manning, 2016). Yet it is also from this same space, where the topic, in its indeterminacy may be seen as decidedly unrigorous due to its untimely obscurity (Manning, 2016). At this early point, it has a rather precarious ability to withstand academic scrutiny due to its ineffability. For this reason, it could be overlooked, forgotten, or replaced by a topic or problem external to the event. As if, as Alaimo says, "the world exists as a background for the human subject' (2016, p. 1), a world full of contents made available for the pickings of the human. Conceptualising a research topic can be a gradual process where both problem, phenomena and researcher are simultaneously composed. It is through intuition that a problem's pulse can be felt in event time. Intuition is a form of knowledge which can be hard to defend, yet as Manning argues, "intuition is a rigorous process that agitates at the very limits of an encounter with the-as-yet-unthought" (2016, p. 33). If I must start at the beginning how can I start experimenting with whatever has the sufficient processual allure (Manning and Massumi, 2014); paying attention to the rumbling vibration of the proto-political; thinking through colour and texture; all whilst embracing an ethics of hapticality (Harney and Moten, 2013), and tenderly sensing through the materiality of my emerging topic?

Three and a half years ago

> I'm asked to bring an 'object' with me to a collaborative writing group. I think my way around the house and pick out what stands out to me, anything. I gather everything up, all matters of things, take them out to the garden, and lie them down wherever they want to lie. I don't know why I do that. Some roll away or leak onto the grass, or stab the earth. I lie down with them. Again, I don't know why. But I stay a while.

I wonder about my own ability to carry out a piece of research and to meet expectations: my own mainly. I will myself to be more pragmatic. Massumi explains: "For out of the pressing crowd an individual action or expression will emerge and be registered consciously. One "wills" it to emerge, to be qualified, to take on socio-linguistic meaning, to enter linear action-reaction circuits, to become a content of one's life-by dint of inhibition"' (1995, p. 91). Yet despite my good 'intentions' as soon as I ask myself where I stand in relation to my project, what position am I taking, I seem to halt the process of the inquiry. But what I hadn't realised was that by focussing on the here-and-now, by lying on the grass together with 'my data', I had been pragmatic of sorts; or at least pragmatism had occurred, cuts had been made. But this pragmatism was of the nature of a more delimiting, speculative pragmatism (Manning, 2016). It allows me to stay at the very heart of the processual possibility, without putting pressure on it and getting in the way; experimenting in the here and now whilst staying committed to the not-yet-known, or the more-than, where questions of becoming remain over questions of knowing (Grosz, 2017).

As I lie on the grass, listening, I realise how noisy it is; revving and screeching. It is urban. I try not to interpret but there it is; the thunder of engines, and the screeching of brakes. Interpretation happens so quickly. Maybe it is my interpretation, but I don't feel like it stemmed from me. A coffee cup rolls to my side and spills dampness onto the earth beneath my elbow. I am startled. A motorbike ran me over, stunning me and overwhelming my perception and asking me why I am standing in the road. Didn't I know it may be dangerous here? Now I wonder if I should go back inside. As I try to get back up onto my feet I hold on to the sides of hapticality. Hapticality being

> the ability of all to feel into and across the unforeseeable potentials existing within even the most violent and modulatory landscapes. To be haptic is to move with the modes of attention that an event needs, at the meeting point of the ever singular differences that weave the texture of the experience. [. . .] Stretched over this exciting and intimidating landscape, we feel f(r)iction: the interaction of a troubling, a movement" (Gendron-Blais, Gil, and Mason 2016, p. ii).

My view of the landscape is veiled by a black fog or black cloud of dust. I can't see clearly enough where the next revving engine is coming from, rendering the field even more intimidating; it could hit me from any angle and at any time. As I wipe soot from my eyes I can barely see a substance shifting, out of focus but appearing to move to a different rhythm from the engines and brakes. Rural perhaps. Summer breeze. A tender touch, a gently whispering melody, pale yellow. It seems absurd against this particular milieu and its point of difference captures my attention and pulls me toward its delicate and ashen song. Perhaps this tenderness was its own silent scream of 'see me,' 'hear me', 'feel me', directed out to the uncultivated field. The black dust cloud rumbles a threat of oozing operation and, as I turn, it enters my body through aligning its pulse-breath with mine; in the end maintaining my intimacy and revving me up alongside it, so as I am alert, ready, affecting my capacity to act, a resonance with the oozing operation. I stretch out my hand, a meek gesture towards the melodic song but by now my energy is too high for the fragile sound. The black cloud spits black dust over the top of it, contaminating and dominating it, obscuring its song until it is harder to hear then rises on its back wheel and comes towards me at full speed. I brace myself and inhale before holding my breath as it grabs me and moves through me once again. Its dust folds into the fissures at the back of my trachea. I try to wipe its traces of soot from my eyes. The sun goes behind a cloud and I shiver and try to warm myself as a black cloud leaks into my veins, chills my bloodstream, and then dwells for a while. The intensity is both dynamic and compelling but not pleasurable. I move back indoors with the black cloud settled in my gut. What is this black cloud I wonder, losing sight of pale yellow, and wondering what does it want? As Maggie MacLure says:

> Wonder is not necessarily a safe, comforting, or uncomplicatedly positive affect. It shades into curiosity, horror, fascination, disgust, and monstrosity. And the particular hue or tenor that it will assume is never entirely within our control. But the price paid for the ruin caused—to epistemic certainty and the "sedentary" achievement of a well-wrought coding scheme or an "arborescent" analytic framework—is, according to Massumi (2002, p.19), the privilege of a headache. Not the answer to a question, but the astute crafting of a problem and a challenge: what next?' (2013, p. 229).

What next? I have begun to pave the way, begun to craft a problem but still my project is, as yet, not ready to tune to language. Would it sound at all legitimate to say that I am researching a fog or black cloud? Or should I just make something up? Pluck something from thin air? It may not have the same rigor but it would at least save me from the anxiety of not-knowing. It is only now with some hindsight that I know that at that point I was still eleven giant steps away from being able to answer questions as to what I was researching. The eleven steps looked something like this:

    Black Cloud

    Plack Cloud

    Plank Cloud

    Plank Rloud

    Plankgrloud

    Plankgrlohd

    Poankgrlohd

    Poankgrolhy

    Poankgroahy

    Pornkgroahy

    Pornogroahy

    Pornography.[1]

Black cloud tentatively (and at times aggressively) individuates and emerges as pornography. This process may go some way to illustrate that I did not exactly *choose* this topic or cherry pick it, but I was in fact experimenting with the pornographic milieu long before I *knew* I was dancing, and at times being run over with and by this phenomenon. If I could have picked my topic, resonated with anything at all, I admit to thinking at times that I would not have picked the pornographic cherry from the tree. Viewing it as all too risky or exposing to me as researcher, revealing both my proximity, wonder, and interest in this topic and for pulling the unexpectant reader in to being complicit with me. I would have perhaps wondered about how some might view my topic. Susanna Paasonen says that it is "the critic's point of view that tends to dominate in porn studies" (2017, p. 3), and explains that this is due to people's activist and institutional passions surrounding it. I agree with her; although my focus too is on the affective rather than a clear and certain feminist position, the topic, by its very nature, can rub up against others in provocative ways, shooting past them or at times even crashing into them (Seigworth, 2016). I may have gone with the phenomena which was singing a sweeter melody, pale yellow. I'm sure it would have had much potential and complexity of its own.

Sound byte

> **A** - You know; I think you always have to grieve the projects that you don't write before you settle on what you do write.

> **B** - Why must we grieve the projects we don't write? They are alive with potential. It would make much more sense to grieve the projects that we do write.

At this time however, it was pornography that was 'fielding' (Manning 2013, p. 2), and it was what felt most resonant and moved me into action. It would seem that working with affect theory and dancing with its forces, and in turn being produced by it as a researcher, means that the unexpected politics that emerge from inside of the process stun me so as to throw me into a shaky and mobile positioning, an insecure and wavering ontology. I am left to steady myself by holding on to the wobbly table upon which affect has squarely placed politics. Kirby and Wilson suggest that my political task is to "think the always/already of our entanglements and intra-implications" (2011, p. 228) in a way that I may not have been able to should I have chosen a topic, even a very political topic, seemingly external to this process. And for this reason I feel a certain sympathy for, and affirm pornography as, 'my' topic. I am in praise of its insurgent qualities, and its ability to remain speculative and forward-thinking. Pornography, as it follows lines of desire, becomes a pioneer of new fields and new imaginings, and I am in praise of its ability to quiver and tremble at the edges of thought. There has been a parallel process for my thesis; in its coming to be, it has gradually taken the form of a pseudo-porn site, and will not be submitted in the paper form I had expected it to be. This may be a first in my department and I affirm pornography's potential to move into new modes of existence, and to continuously create new forms and concepts. I take full responsibility for my research project but not for the subject itself. As Gilles

Deleuze says, "To affirm is not to take responsibility for, to take on the burden of what is, but to release, to set free what lives" (1983, p. 174). That said, I can get in touch with something more stoic in me when I find myself in the company of those who are perhaps not as at ease with my topic as others. As Grosz explains the stoics never underestimate an individual's responsibility as "an individual's actions come from what he or she has 'in them' as part of their character, what they cause in themselves" (2017, p. 27). At times, I thoroughly embrace working with a provocative phenomenon, and I do not wish to dampen how exciting this can be, but my ambivalence lies around the potential negative impact on me: for what I am about to find out, could be seen as thinking with the taboo.

Email exchange

○○○ INCOMING

Hi Fiona,

Mark here. Sorry for disappearing on you there. I've had an idea. How about instead of sharing our projects or watching the films, we put together a little working group. There are some guys over here who are researching some of the more taboo research areas like yours and they will probably have similar issues to you around disseminating knowledge. Maybe we could discuss some of these issues?

What do you think?

M

It is true that I thought this working group could potentially be pretty generative and it is helpful to feel the support and solidarity of those facing the same issues but, at the same time, there was a loss for each of us to be the motley crew of dissidents, under the umbrella of a supposed taboo. And more than this, I had not previously thought of researching pornography as researching the taboo, especially as there are now peer reviewed journals such as *Porn Studies* which are dedicated to this theme, this email was the first time I had been so conscious of the potential my topic had of being received in this way. In many disciplines, this is a battle that has been largely fought and won already and many researchers in the field have paved the way for myself and others so that citing them brings standing to my work. Yet, in some areas this is an ongoing issue. Transversal modes of thought and capacious journals and conferences help this issue by cutting across these disciplinary barriers.

When I hear the word taboo, I read this as a resistance to what is happening in academia with regards to power-knowledge, as opposed to the genre of pornography outside of academia, and I hear it as marking the differences in speed, and the asymmetry between the university and pornography itself. As Manning (2017) explains, the university is a slow-moving machine, not structurally capable of moving at the speed of thought whilst pornography itself speeds ahead taking us to the edges of our knowing.

In the word taboo, I hear a question around what kinds of bodies, what kinds of knowledge and what kinds of experience sustain norms that can so often be upheld through questions of quality and rigor (Manning 2017). And it seems that it is at the specific moment when these knowledges and bodyings take on an (un) recognisable form that they can be erased or removed. From my email exchange, I am left with questions around what kind of knowledges can be truly heard, and what bodies may act as the purveyor and guarantor of what counts as experience and knowledge in a university (Manning 2017).

If taboo means improper or unacceptable, prohibited, excluded or forbidden, then this would capture an albeit small part of my experience of studying this phenomena: after all it had been difficult for me to find those who would help me to build a pseudo-pornography website, or to act in or produce films with me which contained background explicit material from a website. Yet sometimes being with others who are under the same umbrella, in the way Mark suggested in his email, can be easier.

Nearly a year ago at a conference the chair of my panel introduces me:

> 'And now we welcome Fiona Murray from University of Edinburgh. I'm sure she will be the climax of the panel today as she brings her paper, "Online Gonzo Pornography: Feminist Struggles".

Laughter: I walk up to the front.

There was no resistance to my topic in the beginning, before the study was named. Now, resistance can be found hidden in the inflection of the introduction at a conference, or the force of the joke made to 'lighten' the academic atmosphere. This policing can come in the form of sniggers, furtive glances, and on occasion, the odd dismissive sneer. It is not that I am against some humour. And I do understand the specific provocations of 'my topic'. I want my topic to play and not act in a supercilious manner. Yet at the same time I would also like it to be met seriously, and for others to tease out its complexities and make sense of its embedded trajectory (Alaimo 2016). And most of the time my topic is met with sincere interest. But when I am introduced at the conference as the 'climax' of the panel, I go through a kind of subjectivation process (Michel Foucault 1982) where I am more than the amp, or the conduit, for expression but rather a phenomenological subject whose project is about *my* direct experience rather than about *our* entanglements of which we are all a part. And if the climax happens during the second of the six speakers, this makes for a rather long post-coital phenomenological love-in.

At the same time, during this panel, I performed an auto-ethnographic piece which is no mean feat, and not without its tensions when embracing a new materialist lens, and so in many ways I encouraged ideas of my own solipsism in order to challenge it. In my own mind, I referred to this as my ethno-autography where I recognise the entangled nature of my own transcorporeality, whilst putting the ecology and the field of which I am already (t)angled first (Seigworth 2016). This seemed to pay due respect to the knowledge that "the human has become sedimented in the geology of the planet" (Alaimo 2016, p. 3), and at the same time recognised my own coming to be as the architect of my research. It felt like an effective practice where experimentation can play in the void, with all its exposures and vulnerabilities and pleasures. The 'I' being interface with the ecological aspect of ourselves, a superject (Whitehead, 1927), where experience is not belonging only to the human. My ethno-autography pays minute detail to how an individual comes to stand out as one from a broader field of activity (Massumi 2013, p. xi). It is not an 'I' of a singular, localised subject but a tentative expression towards an 'autie-I', a heterogeneous, neurodiverse 'I' which embraces the production of the whole; connecting the human, the nonhuman and the more than human, where there is always more than one, more than two. As Manning says, "the relational is everywhere active in the writing, a language we can also become attuned to in the complex fieldings of choreographic thinking, in the dance of attention, in architectings of mobility that create propositions for an ecology of participation that exceeds what we thought movement could do" (2013, p. 185). It pays close attention to the work of the hyphen (autie-I) asking once again with Manning, "in what ways does the hyphen make operational interstitial modes of existence?" (2016, p. 11).

In the future

I find myself on a panel again at the next conference. So as to avoid a similar disparity (hilarity?), this time I am with others who 'chose' similar topics. Just like when I go to visit Mark I shall meet with others who have perhaps 'chosen' similar taboo topics. Choice is something that is celebrated by neoliberal feminism, celebrating a woman's 'choice': choice to objectify herself should she wish, or to choose a taboo topic should she wish, and that if I don't want to be met with such issues then I should 'choose' another cherry from the tree. As Michaele Ferguson says, "This focus on individual freedom, choice and autonomy is what undergirds new-liberal feminist ideology: women should respond to gender inequality by making better individual choices" (2017, p. 59). Such 'choosing' takes the political back off the wobbly table again.

Is there a loss to this making-coherent (rational) of the panel? How can conference panels be more capacious and work so as not to collapse divergence into coherence and consistency and into restrictive limits, ensuring "consensus and inclusion in advance of political action" (Ferguson 2017, p. 53)? How can they work to maintain the hyphen in order to see its effects across the different papers and disciplines?

Now

As I near the end of the creation of my research project I contemplate that — should I actually have the choice, if what I could choose was distinguishable from the choice (Deleuze 1986), would I continue to work with my pornographic cherry? I'm not sure, but if I do then I hope for capacious conferences and journals with my own words, and (t)angles through engagement and participation in a "creatively productive fugitive zone. . . (where) we might practice the arts of divergent, tapestried becomings" (Joy and Fradenburg 2016, p. 168). And I would do it for the reasons offered by Rosi Braidotti: "for the hell of it and for the love of the world" (2006, p. 259).

I start to pack up my things. I've been at the office on the top floor all day. An office of around forty hot desks. I like desk number twelve. I wonder if anyone would mind if I left a couple of folders on the table since I'll be back in early tomorrow morning. No. I better not. I put them in the locker, clearing all traces. I wonder if anyone else will sit at 'my' desk today and what they will be writing about. The door closes behind me and I wait for the lift. Someone is just arriving. We say 'Hi' as we pass. They enter the office and sit down at desk number twelve. The seat is still warm. They take out their folder and log on to the computer. They wipe the black dust from the keyboard and a little bit of soot gets under their nail.

Endnotes

1. The idea for this word-play came from a presentation by Helen Palmer (2016).

References

Alaimo, S. (2016). *Exposed: environmental politics and pleasures in posthuman times.* Minneapolis: University of Minnesota Press.

Braidotti, R. (2006). *Transpositions: On nomadic Ethics.* Cambridge: Polity Press.

Deleuze, G. (1983/2006). *Nietzsche and Philosophy.* London: Continuum.

Deleuze, G. (1986). *The Movement Image: Cinema 1.* Minneapolis: University of Minnesota Press.

Ferguson, M.L. (2017). Trump is a Feminist and Other Cautionary Tales for Our Neoliberal Age. *Theory and Event*, 20 (1), pp. 53-67.

Foucault, M. (1982). The Subject and Power. In: H.L. Dreyfus and P. Rabinow, eds. *Michel Foucault: Beyond Hermeneutics and Structuralism.* Brighton: Harverster, pp. 208-226.

Fradenburg, L.O.A. and Joy, E. (2016). Unlearning a Dialogue. In Dunne, É. and Seery, A., eds. *The Pedagogics of Unlearning.* Punctum Books. Available at https://punctumbooks.com/titles/the-pedagogics-of-unlearning [Accessed 17.4.2017].

Gendron-Blais, H., Gil, D. and Mason, J.E. (2016). An Introprocession. *Inflexions 9: F(r)ictions,* pp. i-vii. Available at www.inflexions.org

Grosz, E. (2017). *The Incorporeal: Ontology, Ethics, and the Limits of Materialism.* New York: Columbia University Press.

Harney, S. and Moten, F. (2013). *The Undercommons: Fugitive Planning & Black Study.* New York: Minor Compositions.

Kirby, V and Wilson, E. A. (2011). Feminist conversations with Vicki Kirby and Elizabeth A.Wilson. *Feminist Theory* 12(2) pp. 227-234.

MacLure, M. (2013). The Wonder of Data. *Cultural Studies ↔Critical Methodologies,* 13 (4) pp. 228-232.

Erin Manning: Performances of Neurotypicality, Acts of Neurodiversity (2017). [Video]. Manning, E. Available at: https://vimeo.com/218116431 [Accessed 20.6.2017].

Manning, E. (2016). *The Minor Gesture.* Durham: Duke University Press.

Manning, E. (2013). *Always More Than One: Individuation's Dance.* Durham: Duke University Press.

Manning, E. and Massumi, B. (2014). *Thought in the Act: Passages in the Ecology of Experience.* Minneapolis: University of Minnesota Press.

Massumi, B. (1995). The Autonomy of Affect. *Cultural Critique,* 31 (Autumn), pp.83-109.

Massumi, B. (2002). *Parables for the Virtual: Movement, Affect, Sensation.* Durham, NC: Duke University Press.

Massumi, B. (2013). Prelude. In Manning, E. *Always More Than One: Individuation's Dance.* Durham: Duke University Press, ppix-xxiii.

Paasonen, S. (2017). *Writing on Porn* [Blog] Susanna Paasonen. Available at: https://susannapaasonen.org/2017/04/03/writing-on-porn/ [Accessed 17.4.2017].

Palmer, H. (2016). Diffractive Writing Practices: from Barad to Blackpool. Conference paper presented at *Debates in New Materialisms II: Feminism, Politics, Corporealities, Onto-Epistemologies.* London: Central Saint Martin's University of the Arts, London.

Seigworth, G, (2016). Capaciousness. [online] Available at: wtfaffect.com/capacious [Accessed 17.4.17].

Whitehead, A.N. (1927.1985). *Process and Reality: An Essay in Cosmology.* New York: The Free Press.

Williams, D. (1998) *Autism and Sensing- The Unlost Instinct.* London: Jessica Kingsley. Kindle Version.

Thimble Fingers

Kay Gordon

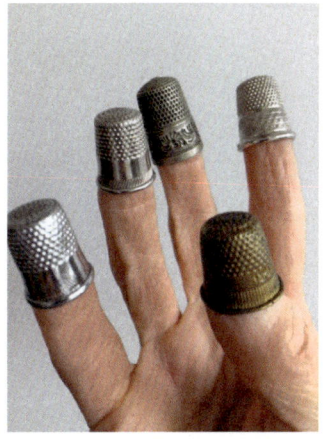
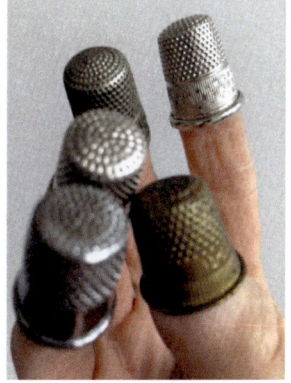

An unintended collection—I've somehow inherited from most of my female relatives (great-aunt, both grandmothers, stepmother, mother). I was goofing around in the studio when I took these photos, after I did a big spring cleaning.

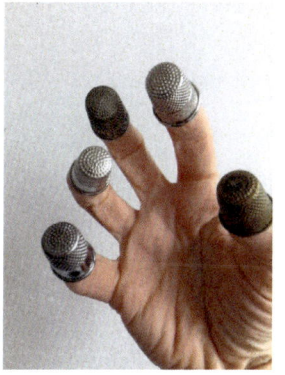
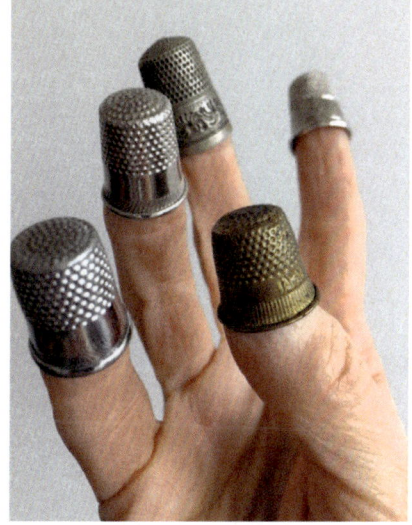

Looking at them later, I realize they feel very connected to feminist hygiene. Like armor for women's work. It's always the play with materials, maybe the "intra-action" that manifests what I didn't know I knew. Doing as knowing/making as knowing, I guess.

Feminist Hygiene

Kay Gordon

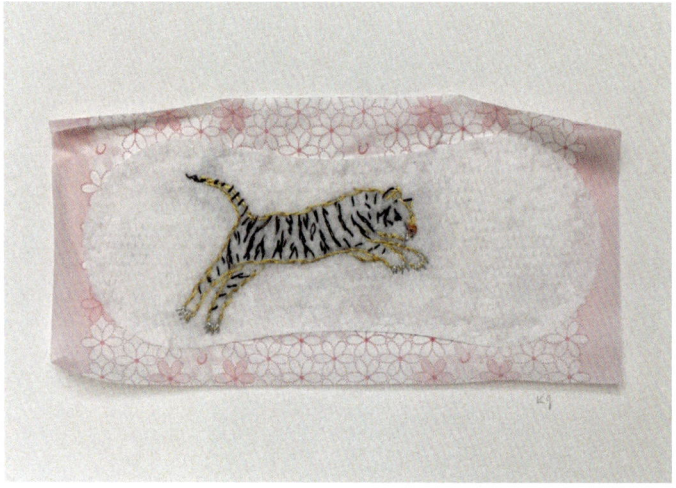

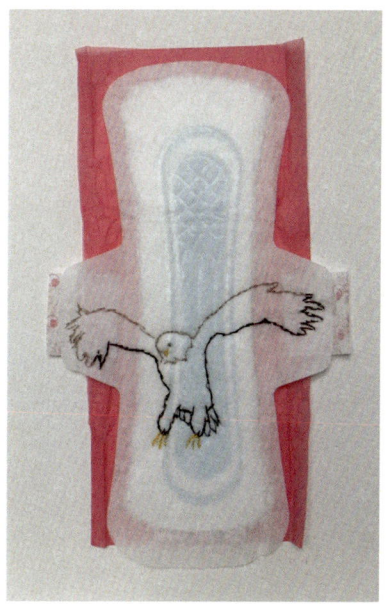

Everything Initiates

Katie Stewart
UNIVERSITY OF TEXAS AT AUSTIN

Untitled, Tom Hsu, 2017

Everything initiates

In my hotel hallway in Boulder there's a framed photograph of Bob Dylan's face above an antique table and a vase of flowers. The handwritten caption reads "All I can do is be me, whoever that is." The claim to a centering self prompts an anxious jolt, the passing recognition that the "me" is a mass of reactions. The self is not the kind of thing that just declares itself. It's what likes to swim, what gets dreamy at the glimpse of a scene on the side of the road, what prefers strawberry jam on its toast.

Surprise

Surfaces take on traction in the ordinary generation of phenomena (as in "When did tattooing your head become a thing?"). Sociality is an info-botic query into what others know. "How'd you get into *that*?" "What *is* that?" The mode of surprise is not only because of the conspiracies and occluded zones but because whatever has popped up is so specific to an angle, or a mood, or a competency and being "in" it, even in passing, is a commitment to the activation of the details of some world you didn't even know existed.

Under Pressure

We live in an "as if", "so what" world, outsiders to the mechanics of how things work. Sociality is under pressure. Composites of money and impacted bodies are the taught tendons of the affective, energetic, material world. Ecologies of living compel manic labors of keeping up with what's at hand but most of us are also bowled over by the torque of things. The punishing realism of so-called "best practices" gestures, cynically, at the vague notion of an upright centering. Noumena now touch matter as a matter of course. There may be the cohesion of a milieu or a habit entrained, for better or worse.

Untitled, Tom Hsu, 2017

Weight of the World

We hope for and fear the weight of the world. We're selfie-obsessed or hoarding. Or we're all about mindfulness achieved and hardened against the situations of the others. Things provoke us; we're barely bearing up. We rage up from an unsteady place to an overwhelm in a hundredth of a second. Or we labor at athletic yoga that takes us all the way down every day. Too many get a shit storm of a life and then have to find ways to get to the food bank on top of everything else. Unmarked white-collar criminals push through the sinking bodies; their own crazy is now their only, lonely undertow.

Preparations

Evan Osnos's piece in *The New Yorker,* "Survival of the Richest: Why Some of America's Wealthiest People are Prepping for Disaster", announced that fifty percent of Silicon Valley billionaires are now survivalists (January 30, 2017, p 37-45). Hedge-fund managers in New York are into it too. The top one percent trade in probabilities. They know the chances that nothing breaks in the next fifty years in a network of nested risk factors: the food supply depends on GPS, which depends on the internet, which requires the grid, towers, underground and undersea cables, software. Ricocheting between techno-optimism and the apocalypse that pings off grotesque inequality, ecological disaster, bad connections and rogue elements, they think of everything. They stockpile gold, Bitcoin, cryptocurrency, and real estate. Lasik surgery frees them of the need for contact lenses or glasses in the event of a crash. A militia would have to be formed; they see themselves as leaders of a community. Like the moneyless Preppers, whose apartments are survivalist storage units and who dream of buying land on the gulf coast and a railroad car to live in, they have motorcycles to move through the traffic jams of fleeing cities. The preparations - food canning, real estate shopping, shooting practice - are ways of breathing, as in "take a breath."

Untitled, Tom Hsu, 2017

It's pragmatic for them to invest eleven percent of their hyper income on land in New Zealand (first world, self-sufficient, and far, far away from the rest) or a three-million-dollar luxury condo in a nuclear-hardened 1960s underground missile silo in the desert tricked out with highest end fixtures, manufactured natural lighting and air, and LED "windows" offering real time views of the prairie above or Central Park. In the event of a disaster a swat-team armored tank will pick up any owner within a four-hundred-mile radius. There's a sniper roost built into the top of the silo and floors of public space below: a spa, kitchens, meeting rooms, a gym, a track. Solar panels, tilapia farms, elaborate filter systems, and hydroponic vegetables expand the self-sufficiency of the underground living. They've planned to avoid depression (more lights) and prevent cliques (rotate chores).

The Women

The women in customer service keep asking me, "512, is that an *area* code? From Texas? Oh, I feel sorry for people who have to live there, what is it now: tornadoes, floods, what's the *temperature*?" As New Englanders, they also believe in social services, so *not* Texas. But what's happening here is a national conversation lite about living right in the middle: not too much of this, not too little, not too far or too close. It's as if everyone's joined the local booster club, and, for a minute, excess and the sad are somewhere else. A deliberate collective fiction that leans into a joking, but also squares on a straight-up loyalty to the good that's in between.

George's daughter, Mary, plops herself down in a chair at the kitchen table for a little visit because she thinks Peg and I are a trip. She says she has to get back to work but she's getting a beer. She's working for a criminal defense attorney doing his shit work until she gets clients of her own. Some asshole beat the crap out of his girlfriend and Mary's come up with an argument that the 911 call is inadmissible because the statement "he choked me" is not an *imminent* threat but a *past* threat. She hates the work but she's also getting a charge out of the game. Part of me wishes I wasn't here, but on the other hand I've never been inside a lawyer's head before. Peg, though, has had enough of all *this*. She responds to whatever people say with "Ya, I get *that*" but she says it just a split second before they've finished their thought because she knows where it's going. She's signaling a kind recognition, a being on their side, but also a wise-ass, Buddhist, disavowal booby trap that says let it go, zip it up, move on, that's enough of that.

I was in the state liquor store stocking up on tax-free social liquor for the summer. I invented a game for my then 12-year-old, asking her to carry a great big bottle to the cash register. The clerk started screaming at me that this was illegal in the state of New Hampshire and they could take my house, they could arrest me, and I'd be in jail. When eye contact with the clerk didn't get her to stop, I turned to the now extremely anxious child to insist loudly and slowly that none of this was actually going to happen, not ever, and the clerk burst into tears. "Oh honey, no! You didn't do anything wrong! No, no no!" This was a time for dramatic pause but we were out of there.

Meanwhile

Meanwhile, back on the academic ranch, the death maws of humanist critique just keep snapping at the *world* as if the whole point of being and thinking is just to catch it in a lie. As if some fixative of state power or normative fantasy could be the *only* problem. As if there's something *wrong* with other people. Some of the things this view misses: all the extensions of ways of being touched, what it feels like to be carried along by something on the move, the widespread joking, the voicing, the dark wakefulness, the reluctance, the stuckness, the sonorousness, how managing a life vies with an unwitting ungluing, how things get started, how people try to bring things to an end, like the day, through things that slam or slide down their throats, why thought might become an add-on or window dressing, or take the form of a speed list condensing a range of possibilities, or why it matters that attention sometimes slows to a halt to wait for something to take shape.

So, you're writing. You make a pass at capturing something. It's too fast for you, the world doesn't cooperate, but you get *some*thing. You follow things around, backing up at the hint of a precision, muscling your way in. You see how much you can't catch, especially now that you're onto a composition of your own. You need another detail, you get rid of a container concept that doesn't work. Writing's accordion mechanics of expansion and contraction changes the environment of a concept. Thought becomes a little surprised to latch on to something, to arrive somewhere, still looking around. It turns to what could happen, not what seven things make this scene a clog in some big picture or a chutes-and-ladders shortcut right into its dangerous fantasy.

References

Evan Osnos (2017). Survival of the Richest: Why Some of America's Wealthiest People are Prepping for Disaster. *The New Yorker,* [online]. Published on January 30, 2017, pp. 37-45. Available at: http://www.newyorker.com/magazine/2017/01/30/doomsday-prep-for-the-super-rich.

Untitled, Tom Hsu, 2017

Contributors

SARAH JANE CERVENAK is an associate professor, jointly appointed in the Women's and Gender Studies and African American and African Diaspora Studies programs, at the University of North Carolina, Greensboro. Her current book project, tentatively titled *Black Gathering: A Minor Aesthetic of (Un) Held Life* queries the Black radical, feminist potential of gathering in post-1970s Black literary and visual arts. She is the author of *Wandering: Philosophical Performances of Racial and Sexual Freedom* (Duke, 2014). Her single-authored publications appear in *Feminist Studies, Palimpsest: Women, Gender, and the Black International, Women and Performance: A Journal of Feminist Theory, and Discourse*. She has also co-authored two essays with her friend Dr. J. Kameron Carter in *Women and Performance: A Journal of Feminist Theory* and *CR: The New Centennial Review*. In addition to co-authored writings, Cervenak and Carter conceptualized and co-convened a 2016-2017 Mellon-funded speaker and working group series titled "The Black Outdoors: Humanities Futures After Property and Possession."

KAY GORDON is a visual artist working in Brooklyn, NY, and an instructor and doctoral student at Teachers College, Columbia University. The fundamental themes in her work include the balance of chaos and order, and the dependency of one object's juxtaposition to the next to reveal its form or even create its existence. Gordon's sculptures and installations include drawing - with wire, thread, shadow, on a variety of surfaces and in space. For Gordon, formal composition creates a framework for revealing subconscious concerns, fears and dreams. Her recent work responds to current political, religious, and natural events.

BEN HIGHMORE is Professor of Cultural Studies at the University of Sussex. His most recent books are *The Art of Brutalism: Rescuing Hope from Catastrophe in 1950s Britain* (2017) and *Cultural Feelings: Mood, Mediation, and Cultural Politics* (2017).

TOM HSU is a studio-based visual artist whose practice investigates absence as communicated through the everyday. He lives and works in Vancouver, Canada and holds a BFA in Photography from Emily Carr University of Art and Design.

GRETCHEN JUDE is a Ph.D. candidate in Performance Studies at the University of California Davis and a composer/performer who currently resides on the island of O'ahu. Gretchen's doctoral research explores the intersections of voice and electronics in transcultural performance contexts, delving into such topics as presence and embodiment in live digital audio, language and cultural difference in vocal genres, and collaborative electroacoustic improvisation. Interaction with her immediate environment forms the core of Gretchen's musical practice. An Idaho native, Gretchen lived and worked in Tokyo, Japan, from 1997 to 2005, and in Oakland, California, from 2008 until 2016. She has been studying Japanese music since 2001 and holds multiple certifications in koto performance from the Sawai Koto Institute, as well as an MFA in Electronic Music and Recording Media from Mills College in Oakland. Gretchen also plays shamisen and sings.

ALICAN KOC is a writer, researcher, and musician based in Toronto. He received both his BA and MA in Socio-Cultural Anthropology at the University of Toronto, where his research has focused on affect and aesthetics. Apart from his scholarly and popular writing, he actively pursues his interest in subcultural aesthetics playing in bands, booking concerts, and archiving the history of Toronto's DIY music scene.

MICHAEL LECHUGA is currently a Lecturer in the Department of Communication Studies and teach in the Masters of Leadership Studies program at the University of Texas at El Paso. He is a recent graduate of the University of Denver's PhD in Communication Studies program, and his research interests are migration studies, alien studies, affects studies, rhetorical materialism, and movement studies.

SABRINA LILLEBY is a PhD student at UT Austin who enjoys thinking about space, place and the affects that circulate in these. She has previously studied and written about domestic work in Cairo where she lived the last six years. Her current project seeks to link precarity and mobility in contemporary Cairo.

FIONA MURRAY is a Professional Doctorate student in Counseling, Psychotherapy and Applied Social Sciences at the University of Edinburgh in Scotland. Her research project, drawing heavily on Erin Manning, is an exploration of how affect theory works within in the counseling room with clients who want to explore their relationship to pornography. Fiona is also a practicing psychotherapist, practicing mother, and she has two dogs to which she is their human.

CLAIRE PAUGAM, born 1991, is a French multidisciplinary and nomadic artist, working with intuition as a tool of investigation, and analogy as a creative process. Claire recently graduated from the MFA program at the Iceland Academy of the Arts. She is now a teaching assistant at the Art University of Reunion Island, another volcanic island (East coast of Africa). Throughout her poetic research, she considers the human body as landscape and landscape as human body. Among other exhibitions, Claire Paugam has exhibited at the 5th International Biennale for Young Art, Moscow (2016), curated by Nadim Samman. clairepaugam.com

MERCY ROMERO is Assistant Professor of Interdisciplinary Studies (American Literature & American Studies) in the Hutchins School of Liberal Studies at Sonoma State University. She received her doctorate in Ethnic Studies from UC Berkeley and her bachelor's degree from Barnard College. She is interested in the application of African American and Latina feminist and humanities research methods in the study of space and society. Presently, she is also working on a book about her hometown, Camden, New Jersey, as a place to think about vacancy, dispossession, and the making of public memory.

JOEY RUSSO is an ethnographer working on queer ecologies, gay conservatism, and incommensurable affects in the American South. His year of fieldwork research in Southeast Texas hanging out in casinos, trailer parks, and grocery stores led to the composing of this piece. He is a PhD Candidate in Sociocultural Anthropology at the University of Texas, Austin.

KATIE STEWART writes and teaches on affect, the ordinary, the senses, and modes of ethnographic engagement based on curiosity and attachment. Her first book, *A Space on the Side of the Road: Cultural Poetics in an 'Other' America* (Princeton University Press, 1996) portrays a dense and textured layering of sense and form laid down in social use. *Ordinary Affects* (Duke University Press, 2007) maps the force, or affects, of encounters, desires, bodily states, dream worlds, and modes of attention and distraction in the composition and suffering of present moments lived as immanent events. Her current project, Worlding, tries to approach ways of collective living through or sensing out. An attunement that is also a worlding. These works are experiments that write from the intensities in things, asking what potential modes of knowing, relating or attending to things are already being enacted and imagined in ordinary ways of living.

AGNIESZKA ANNA WOŁODŹKO holds an MA in Philosophy (UWM Olsztyn, Poland) and MA in The Philosophy of Art History (Leiden University, The Netherlands). She is a PhD candidate in the cultural disciplines at Leiden University. She is investigating ways in which art can, by using living bodies as its medium, reveal the overall cultural, social, and political significance of affect in contemporary understandings of biotechnologically manipulated bodies. She currently teaches in the International Studies program, at Leiden University, and at the AKI Academy of Art & Design, at the University of the Arts ArtEZ.

CONFERENCE

CAPACIOUS
AFFECT INQUIRY / MAKING SPACE
AUGUST 8-11, 2018

Forms Passing, Claire Gilblin, 2016
Acrylic and mica on canvas, 48 x 60"

#*capaciousAIMS*

CAPACIOUS

AFFECT INQUIRY / MAKING SPACE

~~~~

AUGUST 8-11, 2018
MILLERSVILLE UNIVERSITY
WARE CENTER, LANCASTER, PA

This conference has capacious aims! In and across the diverse practices and studies of affect, how might we continue to 'find room' or 'make space' and under what circumstances might such a framing for affect study be problematic? In August 2018, let's meet up and endeavor to find out.

Modeled on the same ethos of community building, mentorship, and intellectual generosity that guides *Capacious: Journal for Emerging Affect Inquiry*, this conference will be open to all (students, faculty, non-academics, and others) while emphasizing the crucial role of graduate students and early-career researchers in shaping the scholarship in affect study.

Like the seriously awesome #affectWTF event of 2015, the three full days of this conference will be largely structured around proposed panel streams. Submissions that tend toward more the un-disciplined, evocative / provocative, and aesthetically-oriented—what we are calling 'interstices'—are also encouraged. Spotlight panel sessions and seminars / workshops with a dozen brilliant up-and-comers, including a few established scholars, will provide stirring evidence and useful insights about the latest trajectories of affect inquiry.

Let's get capacious!!

#capaciousAIMS

MAKE SPACE FOR THESE DATES

- Call for conference stream proposals: November 1, 2017
- Deadline for submission of conference stream proposals: December 15, 2017
- Conference streams decided and posted: January 15, 2018
- Papers and 'Interstices' submission deadline: March 15, 2018

CONFERENCE SCHEDULE

- Opening reception on Wednesday, August 8 from 6-11 pm
- Three full conference days: August 9-11, 2018

QUESTIONS?

capacious@millersville.edu

Of special note/incentive: If you are a published author in the journal *Capacious* by the date of the conference, your registration fee for the conference will be waived

Made in the USA
Middletown, DE
29 July 2017